DIOCESE OF SOUTHWARK

1905 - 2005
A CENTENNIAL CELEBRATION

written by
Revd Antony Hurst

with a Foreword by
Rt Revd Dr Thomas Butler
Bishop of Southwark

and an Afterword by
Canon Eric James

ISBN 0-904129-18-7

SECTION ONE
LONDON SOUTH OF ITS RIVER
South London is Different

London has always, ever since Roman times, spilled over onto the south bank of its river. London's centre of gravity has always been on its north bank, and the Thames has always, even today when there is no reason for it to do so, acted as a barrier, both physical and psychological. But what has spilled over to the south has always been a selected rather than a representative part of the whole. South London has always been different.

London is where it is because of a gravel spit in the middle of the Thames which provided the river's most downstream crossing point, and the first London Bridge was built there by the Romans. Not far upstream was the Horse Ferry, another crossing point, the site of the present Lambeth Bridge. The roads south from London Bridge and from the Horse Ferry converge at London's epicentre, on the south bank because of the river's curvature; always an important roundabout, it is now known as the Elephant and Castle, and it was where south-travelling Romans made their decisions as to whether to head south-east down the Watling Street to Dover or south down the Stane Street to Chichester. So what spilled over the river first were the roads and the travellers, and what spilled over next were the cemeteries because the Romans liked to bury their dead alongside their highways. South London's earliest excavated artifacts are all to do with burials.

And, because of the roads and the travellers and the cemeteries, what spilled over the river next was London's poor; there are Roman remains on the south bank, but nothing that resembles the smart villas that are buried underneath the City. During Saxon times, when the Roman London Bridge had long since decayed and the only means of crossing the river was by ferry, the "Suthvirk" was denigrated as "barbarous". During the sixteenth century John Stow described the main roads in the area as being "lined with the meanest shops and tenements", and the fields behind them as being "pestered with foul cottages and alleys", and at the end of the nineteenth Charles Booth described the southern riverbank from Deptford to Battersea as the world's "longest stretch of unbroken poverty". And, for the same reason that the Romans chose to site their cemeteries south of the river, so the seventeenth century chose to site there its "stink industries", tanning, lead working, manure processing, starching and, later and more curiously, the making of strawberry jam. The docks along the riverside meant that the stink industries' raw materials could be imported and their products exported, and the poor people were there to do the menial jobs both in the factories and on the wharves.

And, because South London was different and because it was poor, something else that spilled over the river was entertainment. A Roman gladiator's trident was recently unearthed in Newington, suggesting it as the site of London's first spectator sports, and throughout the Middle Ages, and probably earlier than that as well, the South Bank was London's red light district. Curiously, the reason for this was that Bankside came under the jurisdiction of the Church. For a thousand years, from St Swithun in the ninth century to Charles Sumner in the nineteenth, South London was part of the Diocese of Winchester, and during Norman times the Bishops of Winchester, powerful politicians as well as leading churchmen, built for themselves a palace on Bankside because it was easier for them to get from there to Whitehall than it was for them to ride up from Hampshire; they dispensed secular as well as ecclesiastical justice, and their law was laxer than that of the civil authorities. The prostitutes of Bankside became known as

"Winchester Geese", Winchester because of their episcopal protection and geese because of the alluring way in which they were said to flap their arms; being bitten by a Winchester goose meant contracting venereal disease. During the reign of Queen Elizabeth I it was on Bankside that London's leading theatres were built and filled to their capacity, once again because different moral rules applied. Cromwell later closed the theatres and drove away the prostitutes, but when the theatres reopened during the more relaxed ambience of Charles II's reign and the prostitutes resumed their *passeggiata*, it was in Covent Garden and Drury Lane. Nevertheless, the South Bank's reputation for entertainment and moral laxity lingered on; the Vauxhall Pleasure Gardens were opened in time for Samuel Pepys to visit them with licentious intent, and the red light district proper moved a little further south to St George's Circus. In the nineteenth century South London was home to some of the most celebrated Music Halls, and the entertainment tradition continues with the Old Vic, once a Music Hall itself, the Royal Festival Hall, the Royal National Theatre, the reconstructed Globe, Tate Modern and the Triathlon Centre in Docklands.

And, because South London was poor, and because it was different, and because different moral rules applied, the area was always notorious for its crime, and also for its prisons. First of the prisons was the Bishops of Winchester's Clink, built to house those who defied their episcopal and secular authority and, in Cromwell's time, Winchester House itself was used as a lock-up. In the eighteenth century one of London's most gruesome spectator sports was going to watch the lunatics encaged at Bedlam, now the Imperial War Museum, and in the nineteenth century there was the Marshalsea, immortalised by Dickens in "Little Dorrit". Today there are Belmarsh, Brixton, Wandsworth and Latchmere House. And the criminality continues too. A recent Bishop of Southwark, comparing the ethos of his diocese to that of neighbouring London, said that London's embodied all the niceties of a polite public school whereas Southwark's was the rough and tumble of a comprehensive playground.

But not everything about South London has been, or still is, different. For one thing, on both banks of the river, there were always the docks. London always was, and still is, a port, and up till the 1960s the docks were the heart-beat of the city, though a heart-beat that was, throughout the twentieth century, becoming increasingly sclerotic. In contrast with most other European capitals which look primarily inwards, London has always looked outwards as well, across the sea to the rest of the world. So London, on both banks of its river, has always been cosmopolitan, and has always been a haven for immigrants. To begin with most of the immigrants were refugees from persecution, Jews from Spain and later Portugal, the unwanted of every persuasion during Europe's Thirty Years War, and Huguenot Protestants from France. There were the sailors, who jumped ship in the docklands and chose, for whatever reason, not to seek another berth; early communities included Muslims from the Eastern Mediterranean and North Africa, and the Chinese. And then, in the eighteenth century, there were slaves. Slaves came to South London from the American and West Indian colonies, most of them either as sailors or as domestic servants, but slave status was never recognised in England (see page 28) so if they absconded they were able to stay; there is a "hue and cry" advertisement from the 1750s offering a guinea reward for the recapture of "a black boy, about thirteen years old, run away in Putney on the 8th inst., with a collar round his neck inscribed 'The Lady Bromfield's Black'". During the twentieth century a multitude more immigrants would come to live in South London, including a great many descendants of the eighteenth century slaves.

And another way in which what is now South London used not to be different was that, up till the middle of Queen Victoria's reign, most of it was rural. William Wilberforce, in his diaries, describes himself tramping across fields to get to the village of Clapham, and from Clapham southwards it was all agricultural farmland dotted with small agricultural villages, farmed in much the same way as the rest of England was farmed. Mediaeval churches, or parts of them, which served what used to be these villages still survive in Plumstead (St Nicholas), Lewisham (St Mary), Carshalton, Addington, Reigate, Banstead, Sanderstead, Beddington, Merton and Putney (St Mary). And there is a very moving description of the vicar of Lingfield near Godstone organising for his parishioners a visit to the Great Exhibition of 1851; they were all instructed to wear their best boots and smocks, and to follow behind him two by two, holding hands, so that they wouldn't get lost because none of them had ever been to London before. Queen Victoria was most impressed by their exemplary behaviour, and their neat crocodile was drawn for the Illustrated London News. And there is a part of the Diocese of Southwark which remains rural today; even the Diocese of Southwark has its cows and horses, and the image of the rough and tumble of a comprehensive hardly fits the Archdeaconry of Reigate. The Archdeaconry of Reigate always tends to get forgotten, and the most embarrassing example of this forgettery happened during the millennium year when all the children in all the C of E denominational schools in the Archdeaconry were presented with a Bible signed by the Bishop, but the Bishop who had signed them, in semiotic error, was the Bishop of Guildford. The archdeaconry even encroaches into Sussex and includes part of Gatwick Airport but, by inter-episcopal arrangement, pastoral care of staff, passengers and planes is vested in the Bishop of Chichester.

South London in 1805

1805, exactly a century before the foundation of the Diocese of Southwark, was the year of Trafalgar. The south bank of the Thames from Woolwich to Battersea was lined with wharves, and just inland from them were the stink industries, interspersed with the slum homes, where cholera was rife, of the dockers and of the stink industries' manual workers. In Woolwich there was the Royal Arsenal, and the impressive military barracks of the Royal Artillery which still remain, and there were naval dockyards at Woolwich and at Deptford. Just south of all this were more respectable dwellings, in particular around the Borough and St George's Fields, with homes for the stink industries' owners and for professional people, some of whom were driven to work over London Bridge. Beyond these, and beyond the reach of the cholera, were the beginnings of grander developments, smart terraces built at the end of the eighteenth century along the arterial roads in Camberwell and Kennington. Croom's Hill and Gloucester Circus in Greenwich and the Paragon in Blackheath also date from this time, and Clapham Common North Side and Church Row in Wandsworth indicate that the trend was widespread; Thackeray's Becky Sharpe had lived in Camberwell in the days when it was still thought to be a good address. Tucked in behind these terraces were new squares, West Square, Cleaver Square and Trinity Church Square, which retain many of their eighteenth century houses, and the elegant suburb of Stockwell was built around 1800.

South of all this were agricultural villages, variously served by three significant market towns, Reigate, Croydon and Kingston. Richmond was being developed for the smarter set, stealing in the process some of Kingston's glory; Maids of Honour Row is an apogee which still remains. Croydon was described as "an unpleasant, muddy place filled with uncouth colliers (ie charcoal burners) from the surrounding woods", but its industrial importance is evident from two surprising developments, the first a railway linking it

Regal Splendour, Greenwich Naval Hospital today.

with Wandsworth built in 1801-3, and the other the Croydon Canal built in 1802-9 linking it with Deptford. Kingston was somewhat more sedate, and its market square is the only one in South London which still survives. Larger villages, all of which have classical churches dating back to before 1800, included Charlton, Lewisham (St John), Camberwell (St George), Clapham (Holy Trinity), Streatham (St Leonard), Wandsworth (All Saints) and Kew (St Anne).

South London was never a haven for the aristocracy. There had been royal palaces such as Edward III's manor in Rotherhithe and Henry VIII's Nonsuch Palace in Cheam, but none of them lasted long and nothing of any of them survives. The only pre-Tudor remnants in what is now the Diocese of Southwark are the Great Hall at Eltham Palace and the outbuildings of the manor at nearby Well Hall. Ham House in Petersham, built in the seventeenth century, is the Diocese's only stately home now visited by the paying public in significant numbers. Kew Gardens draws in more, and it too has royal associations, though its most noteworthy buildings are its nineteenth century glasshouses. The dignitaries who left the greatest architectural mark on the Diocese were, surprisingly, the Archbishops of Canterbury. The Archbishops lived in Croydon, part of their diocese till 1985, and during the twelfth century built themselves there the Old Palace and Addington Palace, but a little later, during the fourteenth, they found it more convenient to relocate to Lambeth, a mere river-crossing away from Westminster and Whitehall. But the most impressive building standing in 1805, and still standing today, is without a doubt the Royal Naval Hospital at Greenwich, built on the site of another of Henry VIII's defunct palaces. The oldest part of the complex is the Queen's House, built by Inigo Jones in 1634 for Charles I, and it was flanked later in the century by more grandiose buildings started under Charles II; these are usually attributed to Sir Christopher Wren, but in fact they took so long to build that much of them was designed by his successors, in particular by his pupil Nicholas Hawksmoor. In 1692, in gratitude for the important Anglo-Dutch naval victory over the French at La Hogue which saw off for good the threat of the restoration of the Catholic James II, his Protestant daughter Mary II dedicated it for use as a hospital for sick and disabled seamen, but since then it

4

has served as the Royal Naval Staff College and it now houses the Royal Maritime Museum, the Trinity College of Music, and parts of the University of Greenwich. Hawksmoor also designed one of the Diocese's most remarkable parish churches, St Alfege's Greenwich. Equally remarkable is the nearby St Paul's Deptford, designed by Thomas Archer, and other classical churches which graced the riverbank in 1805 include three dedicated to St Mary, in Woolwich, Rotherhithe and Battersea, and St Mary Magdalene Richmond. The architectural drawings for St Mary's Battersea found their way to America, and are the origin of the design for a large number of the first generation of churches in New England.

The Invention of Commuting

In 1805, in the middle of the Napoleonic Wars, London was just one of a number of Europe's national capitals, but a century later, during the year that the Diocese of Southwark was founded, it was indisputably the most important city in the world, capital of nation and empire, a world centre for commerce and trade, the hub of the global financial market, and a manufacturing centre in its own right. All this required large numbers of people, and all these people required other people to service them, for example domestic servants, shopkeepers, transport workers and entertainers. And all these people needed somewhere to live. During the second half of Queen Victoria's reign London expanded enormously, both in population and in area. Between 1850 and 1900 the population increased from two and a half million to six and a half, and the built-up area increased proportionately even more, with the south bank absorbing more than its share of the growth. What enabled this expansion to happen was the invention of commuting, and what made commuting possible was the coming of the railways, and the coming of the railways to South London led to the building of a whole semi-circle of new suburbs stretching from Eltham in the east to Putney in the west, encircling the traditionally poor areas along the riverbank and the smarter areas a little way inland.

The Habit of Railway Commuting, London Bridge Station 1958

5

Much of this increase in population was natural because death rates were dropping, especially the death rates associated with childbirth, but most of it was a consequence of inward migration. The vast majority of the people who moved into London were poor; they came from all parts of the British Isles, especially from Ireland, and they came from all parts of the world. Most of South London's incomers settled initially in the slums along the riverbank, and from the slums along the riverbank there was outward migration to the new suburbs. Forster's Education Act of 1870 introduced elementary education for all children, and surprisingly large numbers of the poor children of the South London riverbank were able to benefit from it and to become clerks, and thus to form the basis of a new lower middle class. What enabled them to buy their newly built houses in the suburbs was the invention of the mortgage; the economy was expanding, interest rates were stable, the jobs of the new lower middle classes were secure, and banks were awash with capital and looking for new ways in which to invest it. London's biggest provider of mortgages was the Abbey Road Building Society which later amalgamated with the National, and the biggest in South London was the Woolwich which had begun as a Friendly Society set up for their own benefit by the workers at the Royal Arsenal. A high proportion of today's houses in the Diocese of Southwark were built on the back of this combination of clerking, upward social mobility, mortgages and railways.

The way in which the railways came to South London was, once again, different. North of the river, the places into which Victorian London naturally expanded were, for the most part, semi-rural estates belonging to aristocratic families like the Russells, Dukes of Bedford, in Bloomsbury, the Seymours, Dukes of Newcastle, in Bayswater, and the Grosvenors, later Dukes of Westminster, in Mayfair and Belgravia. Although already rich these families wanted to become even richer, and they knew how to do it; they sold off their land in small plots whilst retaining the ground-leases for themselves, and were thus able to control the size and the design of the houses that got built in a way that kept their ground-rents high. And, in order to maintain these property values, they kept out the railways; King's Cross, St Pancras, Euston, Baker Street, Marylebone and Paddington were all built on the far edges of these estates and at quite a distance from where the people on the trains wanted to get to. So what came next, in North London, was the Underground; the Metropolitan Line was built in 1863 to link all the northern stations, and the network was later extended to carry commuters closer to their places of work.

But in South London it was different because there were no such aristocratic estates. There were estates, for example Telegraph Hill in New Cross, where the homogeneity of the architecture indicates that there was once ground-landlord control, but their one-time owners did not have the power to keep the railways out; indeed they welcomed the railways because the sale of their ground-leases was dependant on commuting. And the absence of aristocratic estates meant that the railways which served South London were able to come right up to the river; London Bridge and Waterloo were built on the river bank, and the lines coming into Cannon Street, Charing Cross and Victoria were able actually to cross it, so that South London's commuters were able to get off their trains much closer to their places of work. All this meant that the spider's web of suburban railways was developed earlier and more comprehensively in South London than in the north, and that the ring of new commuter suburbs soon became solid. London's global preeminence is still nostalgically remembered in its southern suburbia by many of its street names. In 1868 a British Expeditionary Force under the command of Lord Napier invaded Ethiopia and destroyed the fortress of Magdala; there is an Abyssinia Road in Battersea dating from this period, and Napier and Magdala Roads adjoin each other in South Croydon. The Second Afghan War of 1879-80 is commemorated in Clapham by

Afghan Road, Khyber Road, Candahar Road (sic) and Cabul Road (also sic). Berber Road in Clapham reminds us of General Gordon's ill-fated expedition to the Sudan in 1884, as does Khartoum Road in Tooting. Street name memorials to the Boer War are so frequent that to list them would be tedious.

Another consequence of the efficiency of South London's railway network was that it had little need for the Underground. The first tube line to tunnel under the Thames was the East London line linking Whitechapel and New Cross, but more useful to commuters was the City Line linking Waterloo to Bank which opened in 1898. The Northern line from Moorgate to Stockwell, originally called the City and South London, was opened the following year, and the Bakerloo from Baker Street to the Elephant and Castle in 1906, the same year in which the electrification of the Underground was completed which made travelling by tube cleaner, safer, and a great deal pleasanter than it had been in the days of confined steam. Despite the building of the Underground, the commonest form of public transport around the turn of the century was the horse-drawn bus, and an early improvement was the horse-drawn tram; a horse could pull twice as many passengers if the vehicle it was pulling ran smoothly on rails set into the roadway. The first motor buses were introduced in 1900 by the London General Bus Company which pioneered the numbered bus route, and it is amazing how many of the pre-First World War bus routes still carry the same number today, for example the 36 which has been threading its way from Lewisham to Vauxhall Bridge for more than a hundred years.

London's Governance

The foundations on which Britain's nineteenth century wealth was created were the Industrial Revolution and international trade, and during the first half of Queen Victoria's reign a succession of provincial cities, Liverpool, Manchester, Leeds, Birmingham and Glasgow, in that chronological order, rose to positions of eminence. In large measure it was the Mayors and Corporations of these cities who generated their civic enthusiasm and sense of civic identity, and they were able to do so because of arrangements for provincial local government made possible by reforms enacted in 1835. The 1835 reforms, however, specifically excluded London, which was deemed to be a special case requiring special measures. The half-century that followed was filled with sporadic efforts to do something about London's governance, but all of them came to nothing and Londoners suffered as a result. No one was more conscious of this lacuna than the health reformer Henry Chadwick who identified, during the 1850s, the need for a water supply and a sewerage system for London, but he found his plans impossible to implement because there was no competent authority which was capable of taking the lead. In 1854, largely as a consequence of Chadwick's pressure, a Royal Commission was established to consider the government of London, but its conclusion was that London was "a province covered with houses whose diameter from south to north and from east to west is so great that persons living in the furthest extremities have few interests in common. The enormous numbers of the population and the vast magnitude of the interests which would be under the care of the municipal body would render its administration a work of great difficulty". The sole outcome of the Royal Commission was the creation in 1856 of the Metropolitan Board of Works, which pleased no one and excited nobody's imagination, but which nonetheless oversaw a number of crucial improvements to London's infrastructure. One such improvement was the creation of Chadwick's Southern Outfall Sewer, designed and built by one of South London's underappreciated heroes, John Bazalgette, who is buried in a listed grave in Wimbledon parish church.

By the 1880s the provincial cities had had their day and London had reestablished its primacy, and this made the issue of London's governance yet more pressing. The leading advocates of reform had always been the Liberal Party and in particular its Radical wing, the "New Liberal" civic reformers from the Northern cities who were affiliated to the Trade Unions and were the forerunners of the Labour Party. It was, however, Lord Salisbury's Conservative government which established the London County Council in 1888; there had been a financial scandal within the Board of Works and the Government found it more expedient to abolish the Board than to sort out the misdemeanors of its members. Setting up the LCC was a leap in the dark. The Conservative Government had no idea what they were letting themselves in for, and decided almost in passing that London should be a County with the same constitution and powers as Leicestershire or Devon rather than a City like Manchester or Leeds. The first two LCC elections, in 1888 and 1891, were massive victories for the Progressives, a coalition of traditional and "New" Liberals, Fabian Socialists, and other groupings which we would nowadays describe as left-of-centre. Its first Chairman was the future Liberal Prime Minister Lord Rosebery, but the *eminence grise* who actually ran it was Sidney Webb, a Fabian Socialist, a Liberal MP, a Minister at the Colonial Office, and the elected London County Councillor for Deptford. In 1891 he published "The London Programme" setting out his detailed policies, and most of them were swiftly implemented. The LCC's powers were expanded at the expense of other residuary bodies like the Poor Law Boards of Guardians, important services such as gas and water were brought into municipal ownership, and public works were implemented. The most widespread of the early public works was public sector housing; in Webb's own words, "London's poor can only be rehoused by London's collective effort". But Webb's steely left-wing policies alienated a proportion of the electorate, and his ruthless application of the party whip alienated some of the more moderate Liberals. The third LCC elections in 1895 were a close-run thing and the Progressives maintained their power only through the unscrupulous creation of aldermen, and in 1907 they lost control to the Municipal Reform Party, a right wing coalition which was dominated by the Conservatives and committed to minimising the rates.

A phenomenon which Salisbury perpetually dreaded was the spread of "socialism", and he started worrying about the way in which the LCC was exercising its powers, and about the level of public interest that its radical approach was generating throughout the nation. In 1899, in a desperate effort to divide and rule, he asked Arthur Balfour, soon to succeed him as Conservative Prime Minister, to bring in a Local Government Act dividing the LCC into Metropolitan Boroughs. Balfour, since curbing the LCC's powers was his overriding aim, deliberately made no provision for institutional arrangements which might have ensured cooperation between the LCC and its constituent Boroughs but, like so many efforts to divide and rule, his creation served more to embarrass the Conservative Government than to help it. The Boroughs which were controlled by unassailable Progressive majorities, in particular Woolwich, Deptford, Bermondsey and Battersea, used their powers under the Act to implement ambitious programmes of municipalisation, particularly the provision of public sector housing, and all this was perceived by the Government as an anathema to its deeply held *laissez faire* principles, and as further evidence of creeping socialism in action. The Act also, almost certainly without the Government intending it to do so, permitted the LCC to compete with the private sector in providing electric tramways. The LCC used this unexpected power imaginatively in conjunction with its house building programme, and created a large estate at Totterdown Fields in Tooting where, it was proudly proclaimed, every house had a bathroom and an indoor toilet; the estate was served by a tramway which ran north up

Tooting and Balham High Streets. The main private sector provider of electric trams, however, was London United Tramways, and its two hubs were Kingston, which was linked to New Malden, Merton and Surbiton, and Croydon, which was linked to Selhurst, Thornton Heath, Addiscombe and Anerley; the Croydon tramway network has recently been recreated and given a new lease of life.

The Edwardian Era and Armageddon, 1905-1918

The conventional picture of the Edwardian era is of a long hot summer during which ladies carried parasols and young men wore white flannels and straw boaters. This may have been an accurate picture of how a small proportion of Britain's population then lived, but not in South London; as one commentator put it at the time, "ask any gentleman you may encounter walking down the Strand, and he will tell you that, south of the bridges, it is impossible to find either a good tailor or a decent hotel". Life for most people who found themselves in the newly created Diocese of Southwark was very different from the Edwardian image, and very different from what it is today. For one thing, life was short. In 1905 16% of babies died during their first year whereas today's comparable figure is 0.6%, and men now live ten years longer than in 1905 and women twenty. People had to accommodate themselves to death as an everyday experience, and the Book of Common Prayer was speaking literally when it proclaimed that "in the midst of life we are in death". Christianity's promise of an afterlife was a source of comfort to many, but Joseph Chamberlain, after being twice widowed, lost his Christian faith, and David Lloyd George abandoned Christianity after the death of his favourite daughter. Euphemisms were used to soften the blow; it was frequently said that the deceased had "passed on" or "been called away", and the inscription on the tombstone of General William Booth, the founder of the Salvation Army, says that he had been "called to higher service".

But death rate statistics are average figures which conceal a wide variation. The initial population of the Diocese of Southwark split into two roughly equal parts, the poor people along the riverbank for whom the death rates were very much worse than the average, and the upwardly socially mobile people in the new suburbs for whom they were very much better. Life along the riverbank had little to commend it. The first person to collect statistical information to illustrate the extent and the meaning of poverty in England had been Seebohm Rowntree in York in the 1880s, and a decade later his *protege* Charles Booth, no relation of General William, did the same in London. Booth described areas where "every house is filled up with families, and every back garden overbuilt with courts and slums"; sanitation was primitive, and disease rife, particularly tuberculosis to which young women were especially prone. He also analysed income, and found that many families earned less than was needed to buy adequate food; because men's earnings were larger than women's and the family was dependent on them, there was a powerful convention that whatever food was available should go to the men, and women suffered as a result. Many women, especially those deprived by death of a male provider, drifted inexorably into prostitution, and the observer Henry Mayhew has left us a description of the prostitutes in the Cut in Lambeth and in the Borough; "hundreds of them, leaving their parents' homes and low lodging houses every morning, sallying forth in search of food and plunder, a sign not of depravity but of desperation".

And, along the South London riverbank, there wasn't even the working class solidarity that was to be found in the Northern industrial cities; up north, work in the factories and mills, however hard, was at least reasonably secure, and during the early 1900s there was the cohesive glue of Trade Union membership. In South London much of the factory work was seasonal so that income was sporadic, and in the docks, the area's biggest employers, there was a system of "hiring at the gate" which meant that many dockers showed up hoping for work and actually earned nothing. The first major dock strike had been in 1889 led by the fiery John Burns, later Liberal MP for Battersea and a member of Campbell-Bannerman's and Lloyd George's Cabinets; it resulted in the formation of the Dockers' Union but actually achieved little. A significant breakthrough had to wait until 1911 when the dockers again went on strike, forming in the process the Transport and General Workers' Union, and when there was the first national rail strike which led to the creation of the Railwaymen's Union. Even the women factory workers went on strike, and set up their Federation of Women Workers. But, despite these developments, the nostalgia of working class solidarity in South London, which owes much to the security of Trade Union membership, dates from the 1920s rather than from before the First World War.

Meanwhile, in the new commuting suburbs beyond the riverside, a very different culture was being created. In 1908 a remarkable booklet was published entitled "Where to Live Round London"; it sets out details, suburb by suburb, of schools, of golf courses, of local authority rates, and, of course, of train times, fares and frequencies. Most of the early inhabitants of the extensive ring of terraced houses with their stucco and their bow windows were first generation lower middle class, the early beneficiaries of Elementary Education. Most of them did not move out very far, probably only a few miles from where they had been brought up along the riverside, and the common pattern was that a young man would remain living at home throughout his twenties and then marry a neighbourhood girl ten years his junior, take out his mortgage, and buy his new house; later, perhaps, if he did well and got promoted, he might move yet a little further out to an even better address. The husbands commuted into the City or the West End while their wives stayed at home; to have a wife who "didn't need to work" was an important status symbol. Most families had a single domestic servant, often recruited from the area from which the family had initially migrated, and the wife and the servant shared the domestic chores; the proverbial difficulty of having "two women in the kitchen" dates from this time. Domestic service was never popular because of its long hours and semi-slavery status, but for some servants it too represented an escape route out of the slums because of the scope it offered for marrying, say, a suburban shopkeeper. Most children would have gone to the local Elementary School, though private schools were also being created and expanded, and would have left school at fourteen, the boys to start clerking and the girls to help their mothers or perhaps start training as a nurse or a school teacher. Insofar as the phrase "Victorian values" has any worthwhile meaning, it applied to South London's railway suburbs; good behaviour was insisted upon with a fanaticism grounded in a fear of regression back to the slums. The classic literary description of the commuting clerk is George Grossmith's "Diary of a Nobody"; although Mr Pooter lived north of the river in Holloway, he might equally well have resided in Peckham or Putney. The most vivid chronicler of the lower middle classes south of the river, especially in "Anne Veronica" and "Tono Bungay", was H.G.Wells. Immigration and emigration in Edwardian South London, however, were not in balance. More poor people were moving into London than there were upwardly mobile people moving outwards, so some areas which had been built as respectable suburbs became engulfed by poverty, and houses which had been built for single families became multi-occupied. This is what happened in the early years of the twentieth century in areas like Peckham, Camberwell, Brixton, Balham and Tooting.

Then, almost like a bolt from the blue, came the First World War. There is no indication that South London suffered less than its share of the war's casualties, but the effect of its losses was probably less traumatic than elsewhere. Nationally the trauma was felt most strongly by the officer class, and by the industrial cities of the North and the Midlands where the creation of "Pals' Battalions" often tragically meant that large numbers of young men from a smallish area were slaughtered on a single day. Glances at South London War Memorials suggest that the area produced remarkably few officers, and that the "other ranks" were spread amongst a remarkably wide range of different army units. The only infantry regiment with its depot in the Diocese of Southwark was the East Surreys in Kingston, and one of its officers, a Putney insurance agent called R.C.Sherriff, has left us with a memorable picture of what front-line fighting was like in his play "Journey's End". The two most popular regiments seem to have been the Queens Royal Regiment based in Guildford and the Kings Royal Rifle Corps based in Winchester, and the Royal Engineers and the Royal Artillery, which had its depot in Woolwich, also seem particularly well represented. But what is chiefly remarkable about the War Memorials is the sheer number of the names. The nation was determined to remember its dead, and the heroic design of the War Memorials indicates the way in which, officially, this was done. But perhaps more telling memorials are the simplicity of the Flanders poppy which is still worn on Armistice Day, the cynicism of the songs and poetry which the war gave rise to, and the paintings of the official war artists still on display at the Imperial War Museum in Kennington.

On the domestic front the two most important changes during the war's early years were a consequence of actions taken by David Lloyd George when he was Asquith's Minister of Munitions. In keeping with his Welsh Nonconformist background he famously declared, "we are fighting Germany, Austria and Drink, and as far as I can see the deadliest of these foes is Drink". He responded by introducing a maximum alcoholic content for beer and licensing hours for pubs, which included compulsory afternoon closure. Like most of his initiatives it was at first very successful and alcohol consumption dropped by 60% but, unlike most of his initiatives, both these measures remained in force for more than seventy years. And he also sent women out to work. When Lord Kitchener, the newly appointed Secretary of State for War, publicly envisaged the need for a "new army of a million men", Lloyd George responded by signing a deal with the Trade Unions which relaxed all their recently negotiated demarcation privileges, and permitted women to be recruited into what had traditionally been men's jobs. Sepia coloured photographs survive of women driving trams, women being bus conductors, and women working in factories, in particular in the munitions factories around Woolwich. And this had one significant knock-on effect. In South London suburbia, the entire class of live-in domestic servants disappeared almost completely, and almost overnight. In most areas they never came back, though in the smarter parts around Kennington they lingered on for another couple of decades.

Between the Wars, 1918-1939

The prevailing aspiration which followed the Armistice, almost an aspiration of denial, was that life should revert to what it had been like in 1914. In some ways this was manageable, and in others it was impossible. North of the river the aristocracy reverted to its traditional habits, Ascot, Henley and coming-out balls, and unaristocratic South London reverted to its more mundane equivalents, family Sunday lunches and outings to the park. Despite all the First World War deaths there was very little change in the pattern of marriages and births; the ratio of women to men rose only from 107% to

110%, and the birth rate actually increased. And the women stopped working. The Trade Unions held Lloyd George to his war-time pledge; their demarcation privileges were all immediately restored, and the women came back home. But there was one big difference between 1914 and 1918; instead of being the world's wealthiest nation, Great Britain had become effectively bankrupt, in particular because of its indebtedness to the United States. The Government compounded everybody's misery by reverting to the Gold Standard with the pound pegged at too high a rate against the rest of the world's currencies, making the revival of the country's traditional export trade almost impossible, so that unemployment became widespread and systemic. And the Trade Unions compounded the misery for many by protecting their own membership at the expense of the unemployed, successfully campaigning to keep wage rates high and thus preventing prices from falling to an economic level. The aristocracy may have opened up their country houses once again and launched their debutante daughters, but now they were able to afford it only by selling off the family silver. South London didn't suffer as much as did other parts of the country; the diversity of London's job market helped, and so too did the need for the business of government to be maintained. But things were bad nonetheless, though less bad in the commuter suburbs than along the riverside. And something else that changed, understandably enough, was that the pre-war values of duty, service and deference were replaced by a cynicism that ran very deep; insofar as people still had money they started spending it on frivolous enjoyment rather than on serious investment. Aeroplanes became popular for the first time, but more people went to watch flying displays than to travel to anywhere in particular, and where they went to was Croydon Airport where the ghosts of propellered aircraft still haunt what is now an industrial estate. Perhaps South London's best reminders of the frivolity of the jazz age are the *art deco* chinoiserie at Eltham Palace, and the over-the-top decor of the listed Granada Cinema in Tooting.

During the years that immediately followed the First World War, South London's major house builder was the LCC. Economic thinking at the time was dominated by John Maynard Keynes, and his view was that, when times were bad, the Government should initiate projects which would stimulate the economy and create jobs; a South London monument to Keynesian thinking is the extension of the Northern Line to Morden, built more as a make-work project than because it was actually needed. And the LCC followed Keynes's lead. Its now left-wing majority was committed to an egalitarian philosophy which owed much to the dreamy socialism of William Morris, and the houses that were built immediately after the war tend to look like rural cottages; the Well Hall estate in Eltham, on the site of an abandoned munitions factory, is the most enchanting example, and the larger LCC developments of this era include Bellingham, St Helier and Roehampton. The LCC's preoccupations at this time included a distrust of the private sector which meant that its 1920s estates tended to be devoid of shops, and a horror of alcohol; Bellingham was built with one pub to serve its 35,000 inhabitants which compares with a London average of one per 400. It also had something of a blind-spot in respect of schools, churches and other public amenities; its estates were described as being devoid of "soul". But the LCC, perhaps again following William Morris, did understand parks, and it put considerable effort into upgrading its patches of green, for example Peckham Rye, Brockwell Park and Tooting Bec Common.

In the 1930s, once the country had succeeded in negotiating its way out of the Gold Standard, the economy began to revive, and London's economy revived more strongly than anywhere else's. Between 1911 and 1939 the population of the London conurbation grew from 7.25 million to 8.73 million, but all of this increase happened beyond the boundaries of the LCC; the LCC's population remained static, while that of the riverside boroughs, Woolwich, Greenwich, Deptford, Bermondsey, Southwark and Battersea, actually declined as slum clearance and outward migration took their toll on numbers. The sheer quantity of the new houses built in the outer suburbs between the wars, more in the thirties than in the twenties, is staggering, and the contractors who built them are still household names, Costain, Laing, Taylor Woodrow, Wates and Wimpey. The houses were built speculatively, so they had both to be cheap and to sell. They were marketed as rural cottages, but economy prevented them from being detached, so a brilliant compromise was devised; they were semi-detached. Their cottage status required half-timbering, but the exposed timbers had to be creosoted pine rather than oak. Hand-crafted features were introduced like sun-burst front gates and stained glass windows in the hallways, but all these artifacts were mass produced. The *art deco* design might have embodied echoes of post-war frivolity, but what was being offered was serious domesticity. This style of inter-war housing is often referred to as "Kingston Bypass", but it is the dominant design of an entire semi-circle around South London. And these houses have stood the test of time. The number of them that have been demolished during their seventy or eighty year lifetime is minute and, whenever they are vacated, photographs of them never remain for very long on the display boards in estate agents' windows.

The railways continued to provide the basis for outer suburb commuting, but there were a number of new developments. Trolley buses were introduced, particularly around Croydon, but more significant was the arrival of the private car; by 1939 Londoners owned almost half a million of them. In 1923 all the railway companies in South East England amalgamated to form the Southern Railway and, in order to compete with the private car, the Southern Railway immediately started electrifying its tracks, making railway

The Century's Most Revolutionary Weapon, an advertisement from 1933

13

travel quicker, cleaner and more reliable. And the Southern Railway also started promoting real estate, going into business with Costain to help market, in multi-coloured *art deco* posters, the delights of Raynes Park, Motspur Park, Worcester Park, Stoneleigh and New Malden. What was marketed was a lifestyle, a lifestyle as different as possible from the riverside slums; houses were clean and had gardens, and housewives could have their domestic commitments reduced by such labour-saving devices as the vacuum cleaner, the electric iron, and the frigidaire. Some commentators, most notably H.G.Wells, were highly critical of this idealised suburban lifestyle and imagined suburban housewives as trapped and neurotic, but their criticisms were belied by the statistics; families voted with their feet and their mortgages in huge numbers, and the populations of Malden and Coombe, Epsom and Ewell, Sutton and Cheam, Coulsdon and Purley, Surbiton and Banstead doubled during the twenties and doubled again in the thirties. And, by the thirties, the housewives were almost as likely to be working as their husbands; as one commentator put it, "women, in order to free themselves from male domination, left their homes in droves and went out to become personal secretaries".

All this flurry of speculative house building raised another question in people's minds, which was where should London stop. In 1935 the LCC charged Sir Patrick Abercrombie with coming up with an answer, and his proposed solution was the creation of a Green Belt. There is nothing particularly sophisticated about the geographical location of the Green Belt; it is merely a stretch of countryside around the edge of where speculative building had reached in 1935. The concept was nevertheless enthusiastically adopted by the LCC's then leader Herbert Morrison and, quite remarkably, particularly since the LCC had very few powers with which to enforce it, Morrison managed to make the Green Belt stick. The LCC invested heavily in it despite the fact that at that time it was running very short of money; it bought up land in order to ensure it would never get built on, for example Chislehurst Common, Keston Common, Biggin Hill and the Darenth Valley, and it compensated landowners for the loss of the profits they might have expected to make from speculative development. Even more remarkably, the Green Belt is still clearly visible today.

World War II and the New Jerusalem, 1939-1964

The first air raid warning of the Second World War happened within half an hour of Neville Chamberlain's broadcast statement on 3 September 1939 that, because no response to his ultimatum had been received from Germany, Britain was therefore at war. War had in fact been anticipated and precautions put in place a year earlier, in the aftermath of Chamberlain's meeting with Hitler in the Berchtesgarten; gasmasks had been issued, air raid shelters identified, and civilian observers recruited and trained to monitor civilian morale. That first air raid warning turned out to be a false alarm, and the Blitz in earnest didn't start till June 1940. Churchill, in one of his broadcasts which deserves more widespread recognition, described London as "a prehistoric monster into whose armoured hide a shower of arrows can be shot in vain". There are still plenty of people around in South London with stories to tell about their experiences during the Blitz, tragic stories like the bombing of a crowded Woolworths in New Cross in November 1944 which killed 160 people, stoic stories about successive nights spent huddled up with Mum in a cold damp Anderson shelter, sad stories about going home and finding it had been hit, hilarious stories about Auntie being caught in nothing but her underwear, and wicked stories about black market exploitation and coshing in war-dark alleys. And, amongst today's generation of younger pensioners, there are also stories about being evacuated, with identifying labels tied to their overcoat buttonholes, to the unknown and unfamiliar countryside. But the bombing of London needs to be kept in perspective. About 30,000 Londoners died, which compares with over 100,000 in Tokyo and 135,000 in Dresden and, throughout the bombing, ruined buildings were always cleared, the streets were always kept open, and the railway lines were always made good. "London can take it" was the slogan, and take it London did.

And then, between the Blitz and the ending of the war, something remarkable happened. A new spirit started to take hold, a spirit very different from the nostalgia of 1918 which had tried to pretend that the First World War had never happened. It became evident in Government, it became evident in the LCC, and it became evident in the minds of ordinary people. What was wanted, after the war, was something different, something that was cleaner, more spacious, more egalitarian, more efficient, and better planned; a "New Jerusalem", in fact. Much of the dissatisfaction that underpinned this vision was targeted at the lingering on of class privilege, and at the "competitive violence" of private enterprise; the experience of being on the Home Front during the war had brought people together, and together people were determined to stay. Within Government the spirit of the New Jerusalem showed itself in the Beveridge Report of 1942 (see page 49), the Education Act of 1944 (see page 55) and in the National Health Service Act of 1948 (see page 50), and within the LCC it showed itself in Sir Patrick Abercrombie's Greater London Plan. An exhibition was held in County Hall in 1942 setting out the Plan's objectives, and the Plan itself was published in 1945. The mood was set by Herbert Read who famously declared: "When Hitler has stopped bombing our cities, let the demolition squads complete the good work".

The first stage of Abercrombie's plan was the clearance of the bomb damage, but it continued with the clearance of slums and with the replacement of both with LCC housing, enabled and encouraged by the Town and Country Planning Act of 1947 which effectively nationalised development land. The aftermath of the war was a period of acute housing shortage, caused in part by the bomb damage, in part by the needs of the returning troops, and above all by rising expectations. Despite the pressures on him to put quantity above quality, Abercrombie insisted that the LCC's new houses should be built to a high standard, and most of what remains from the late 1940s, for example in Bermondsey, has worn well. In 1951, however, the Conservatives were re-elected to Government, helped in part by Harold Macmillan's pledge to escalate the housing programme, and Macmillan immediately relaxed the Abercrombie standards in favour of a dash for numbers. The inspiration for LCC housing rapidly shifted away from the haphazard rusticity of William Morris which Abercrombie had preferred, and headed off instead in the direction of the geometric brutalism of the tower block in unsubtle imitation of le Corbusier; the Alton Estate in Roehampton, dating from 1955, is a fitting monument to the LCC's obedience to Macmillan's cynical enthusiasm.

Putting out the Blitz, Surrey Docks 1940

The Abercrombie plan also envisaged roads, a spider's web of arterial roads running in and out of London, and a series of four orbital roads linking them christened, with efficiency but little imagination, A, B, C and D. "A" used to be known as the Inner Ring Road, and it gained a new eminence in 2003 when it became, almost exactly, the boundary of the Congestion Charge Zone. "B" is still sign-posted, though not necessarily with much logic, as the South Circular. "C" never got off the ground. And "D", which was to have been around the outside edge of London within the confines of the Green Belt, remained on the drawing boards until 1986 when it eventually materialised, with no acknowledgement of its 1945 provenance, as the M25. Several of Abercrombie's arterial roads were built in North London, smashing their way through houses and shopping streets in the process, but very little actually happened south of the river. South London's High Streets remain on the whole intact, with a high shop occupancy rate, a great deal of retail diversity, and a high proportion of local ownership. A warning of what might have happened had Abercrombie had more of his way can be glimpsed from looking at parts of Purley Way and at the middle section of the Old Kent Road. One almost incidental casualty of the combination of the Blitz and Abercrombie was South London's trams; the tram tracks had been difficult to keep open during the bombing, and Abercrombie saw tram travel as old-fashioned, and London's ultimate tramcar, now preserved in the Covent Garden Transport Museum, rattled its way from Woolwich to New Cross in 1952.

1918 and 1945 had one thing in common in that Great Britain emerged from warfare victorious but virtually bankrupt. Economic activity in the late 1940s was slow and goods were in short supply, and rationing was initially more severe than it had been during wartime; "make do, and mend" remained the housewives' slogan, and children learned the ways of the black economy through trading sweet coupons. For a few years it was possible to continue in the illusion that Britain had retained its former world status; it took time for continental Europe to recover from its far greater war damage, and the habits of Empire preference continued even after a start had been made in winding the Empire up. But by the 1950s it started to become apparent that Britain's standing in the world had seriously diminished, and that so too had London's standing within Britain. Prior to 1950 London, and in particular South London, had experienced a century of almost uninterrupted expansion and enrichment, but the thirty years that followed 1950 were years of almost uninterrupted decline, and a disproportionate share of the burden of this decline fell on South London's riverside. Given that this was what was about to happen, it was ironic that the South London riverside should have provided the site, in 1951, for the Festival of Britain, a heroic attempt at creating the impression that the decline was capable of being warded off (see page 67). Queen Elizabeth II's coronation in 1953 was a similar exercise in illusion, but her rain-soaked procession didn't even bother to cross the river. "You've never had it so good" trumpeted Harold Macmillan in his successful election campaign of 1959, but it was evident even at the time that Britons, and in particular South Londoners, could have had it a great deal better.

A phenomenon which was anticipated neither by the Festival of Britain nor by the Queen's Coronation, and which was to change the whole face of inner South London and have an irrevocable impact on its culture, was Commonwealth immigration. The decade which followed the conclusion of World War II was a period of severe labour shortage; workers were needed to get industry back onto a peacetime footing, the implementation of the Welfare State was creating additional jobs which hadn't existed prior to the war, and the demand for manpower was not yet being offset by the more efficient working practices that came later. But, while there was little or no unemployment in Britain, unemployment and underemployment were chronic throughout much of the

Empire, and throughout much of the Empire social expectations, not least because of the social interaction which the war had generated, were rising fast. Immigration into Britain was the logical consequence, and up till 1962 there was no statutory inhibition on migration from one part of the Empire to another. On 22 June 1948 the Empire Windrush docked at Tilbury with its cargo of immigrants from the Caribbean, and during the years that followed migrants trickled in from India, from Pakistan, from Cyprus, and from throughout the British colonies in the West Indies. Labour-starved employers were pleased to see them and wanted more, and in 1956 London Transport set up a recruitment office in Barbados, and the National Health Service, the British Hotels and Restaurants Association, and many others, followed with initiatives of their own. The reaction in Britain was growing xenophobia, and this exploded into serious race riots in 1958, first in Nottingham and then in Notting Hill. The Conservative Government panicked and gave notice of its intention to curtail the right of abode in Britain of Commonwealth citizens, but the effect of this notice was to turn the earlier trickles into a flood. Tens of thousands of immigrants set out from all over the world in a desperate effort to "beat the ban". Most of the new arrivals went initially to the areas where their compatriots had already settled; Jamaicans went to Brixton and Greek Cypriots to Peckham. And initially they had a very hard time of it. The National Front did its best to fan the flames of xenophobic prejudice by organising marches with placards shouting "Keep Britain White", landlords put up "Whites Only" notices in rooms to let, Trade Unionists went on strike rather than work alongside black colleagues and, most damaging of all, prejudice within the police and the courts meant that the black victims of racial abuse were all too often unprotected by the law. South London, where much of this struggle was played out, was being required to adjust to a completely new set of circumstances. But adjust it eventually did. The earliest arrivals amongst these Commonwealth immigrants are now Old Age Pensioners, and the stories that they tell of the difficulties they encountered provoke in younger listeners sensations of amazement and of shame. But most of these stories are told smilingly because things have since changed, and changed immeasurably for the better, and changed within the life-time of a single generation. South London still has its race relations problems, but few would deny that forty years ago things were enormously much worse (see pages 31 - 34).

Quite apart from all the cultural changes which were provoked by Commonwealth immigration, the early 1960s were also a cultural cataclysm in their own right. If the first half of the forties had been taken up with the Second World War and the second half with surviving the austerity which followed it and with bringing in the New Jerusalem, the fifties were the decade when, with a little more money in their pockets, people started trying to get back to normal. But what was normal? Normal meant a family of Mum, Dad and 2.4 children living in a Surrey suburban semi-detached, behaving well, spending sensibly, and observing all the right social conventions, many of which had their origins in a nostalgia for the thirties. Most people tried very hard to live their lives within this strait-jacket, but it became increasingly evident that the strait-jacket was stretching at its seams. And then, in the sixties when the seams eventually burst, everything started to hang out. The sixties was the decade of liberation, of experimentation, of the Beatles and the Rolling Stones, of hippies, and of sex, drugs and rock and roll. The pronouncements of those in authority were disregarded, social conventions were cast aside, and everybody started doing their own thing. And the sixties was also the decade of "Swinging London". In 1966 the American magazine Time published a leading article which began: "In this century every decade has had its city; during the shell-shocked forties thrusting New York led the way, and in the uneasy fifties it was the heady Rome of *La Dolce Vita*. Today it is London.... London has burst into bloom, it swings, it is the scene". But very little of the

Biba and Habitat culture managed to cross the river. South London did, however, make two contributions to the swinging sixties. One was the battles which were fought out between Mods and Rockers on South Coast Bank Holiday beaches, in particular in 1964, in which a disproportionate number of South London teenagers were involved. And the other, contrary to any reasonable prognostication and which really did swing, was South Bank Religion; Mervyn Stockwood was enthroned as Bishop of Southwark in 1959, and his suffragan John Robinson published "Honest to God" in 1963 (see pages 85-91).

The Sixties and Seventies, 1964-1979

The LCC, for all its good and bad works, had never provided an entirely satisfactory solution to the issue of London's governance. The LCC's boundaries had been fixed at the arbitrary point that house building had reached in 1888, but virtually all the expansion since that date had happened on those boundaries' farther side. The Green Belt had at long last given London an edge, but inside this edge the LCC was responsible for less than half the population and barely a quarter of the land. In 1939 Professor William Robson of the London School of Economics, where he had earlier been a student of Sidney Webb, had published an influential book called "Government and Misgovernment in London". In it he had called for the creation of a Greater London Council reaching out as far as the Green Belt, and for a reorganisation and strengthening of the London Boroughs within it, and also for the abolition of the anomalous powers of the City of London. Robson's common sense solution, however, immediately became the stuff of party politics; the Labour Party assumed itself to be perpetually assured of an LCC majority, while the Conservatives assumed that they would have no difficulty in perpetually winning any GLC expansion which included the outer suburbs. Herbert Morrison, throughout his long tenure as the LCC's leader, opposed any sort of reorganisation along the lines of Robson's proposals, and so did his successor Sir Isaac Hayward who presided over the LCC in the years prior to its eventual demise.

So the initiative in reorganising London's government was taken, as it had been in 1888, by the Conservatives. In 1957 Enoch Powell, then the Minister for Housing and Local Government, established a Royal Commission under the Chairmanship of Sir Edwin Herbert to make the first official recommendations on London's governance since 1834, with Robson as the Commission's advisor. The eventual Herbert Report followed Robson's 1939 recommendations pretty much to the letter, and they were immediately accepted by Sir Keith Joseph, Powell's successor, though with a few important reservations. Successful lobbying ensured that the powers of the City of London remained untouched, and in the interests of efficiency there were to be fewer, bigger boroughs. In inner South London the old Boroughs of Woolwich, Deptford, Bermondsey, Camberwell, and Battersea, all of them with proud histories of left-wing defiance, were swept away, subsumed within Greenwich, Lewisham, Southwark, Lambeth and Wandsworth. In outer South London new Boroughs were created called Bromley, Bexley, Merton, Sutton, Kingston and Richmond, with Richmond straddling the river. Croydon, which had been a County Borough in its own right, retained its former boundaries and became the most populous of the new Greater London Boroughs. Joseph also accepted the important Herbert principle of subsidiarity; the GLC's responsibilities were to be limited to those issues which could not better be undertaken by the Boroughs, in particular with regard to planning. And he also agreed that the LCC should remain an Education Authority, to be known as ILEA.

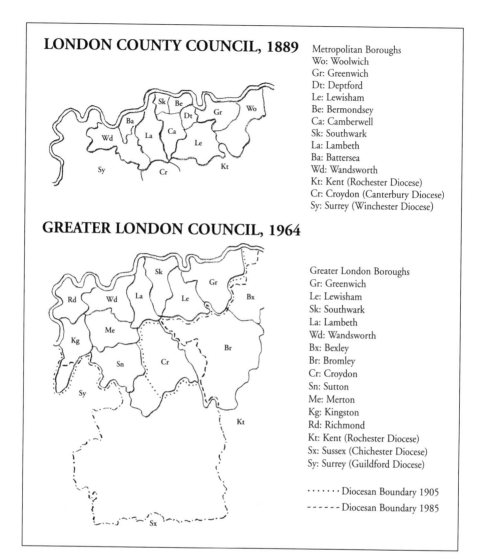

LONDON COUNTY COUNCIL, 1889

Metropolitan Boroughs
Wo: Woolwich
Gr: Greenwich
Dt: Deptford
Le: Lewisham
Be: Bermondsey
Ca: Camberwell
Sk: Southwark
La: Lambeth
Ba: Battersea
Wd: Wandsworth
Kt: Kent (Rochester Diocese)
Cr: Croydon (Canterbury Diocese)
Sy: Surrey (Winchester Diocese)

GREATER LONDON COUNCIL, 1964

Greater London Boroughs
Gr: Greenwich
Le: Lewisham
Sk: Southwark
La: Lambeth
Wd: Wandsworth
Bx: Bexley
Br: Bromley
Cr: Croydon
Sn: Sutton
Me: Merton
Kg: Kingston
Rd: Richmond
Kt: Kent (Rochester Diocese)
Sx: Sussex (Chichester Diocese)
Sy: Surrey (Guildford Diocese)

······· Diocesan Boundary 1905

- - - - - Diocesan Boundary 1985

Then, from Sir Keith Joseph's point of view, two things went immediately wrong. The first was that, in the first GLC elections held in 1964, the voters returned a massive and surprising Labour majority, and the second was that, when this initial Labour majority arrived in County Hall, it permitted the GLC to retain many of the LCC's old powers, particularly with regard to planning. Instead of subsidiarity, there was competition and duplication. The GLC's Planning Department drew up elaborate plans for making Lewisham, Croydon and Kingston "commercial hubs", which probably didn't make any difference to what would have happened anyway, and it initiated some valuable schemes like the building of the Thames Barrier, and it ducked some important issues which it ought to have tackled like the development of the moribund docklands. But chiefly it went on building housing, housing which involved the eradication of the existing street patterns, the removal of industrial and service activities, and the replacement of multiple ownership with municipal monopoly. In the Borough of Southwark alone it was the era of the Heygate, the Aylesbury, the North Peckham and the Gloucester Grove estates. The most scathing indictment of this process was made by Nicholas Taylor in "The Village in the City" (1973) who spoke of "fashionable architects who sit all day at their drawing boards in County Hall designing harsh piazzas for Battersea and Bermondsey, and then, at 4.51 sharp, descend to the tube train, roaring out under the forgotten development areas for which they are responsible till they come to the surface at their own cosy creeper-covered cottages in Wimbledon or Hampstead". And Ian Nairn commented in "Nairn's London" (1966), "of all the things done to London in the course of this century, this softly spoken `this is good for you' castration is the saddest".

Fortunately for South London, the GLC Planning Department didn't have everything its own way, and much of its effort was subverted by events. The first of these subverting events was the Rachman scandal in 1963, when the malpractices of a private slum landlord in his treatment of his tenants were dramatically exposed in banner headlines, coincidentally linked to the goings-on of John Profumo and Christine Keeler. What mattered, however, was not so much Rachman's iniquities as the newly elected Labour Government's over-reaction to them. Anthony Greenwood, Harold Wilson's Minister for Housing and Local Government, swiftly brought in the 1964 Rent Act, giving new rights to tenants and severely restricting the freedom of private landlords. Its effect was to make owning-to-let immediately unattractive; renting from private landlords had long been the mainstay of working class housing along the South London riverbank, and its tenants were much less happy to see their landlords go than were the principled Labour politicians in Government and in County Hall, motivated as they were by dogma rather than by first hand experience. Then, in May 1968, there was the catastrophic collapse of a tower block in Newham called Ronan Point. The effect of this subverting event was to bring home to the planners the point which tower block residents had long been making, that tower blocks were unpleasant and dangerous places in which to live. And the consequence of these two events, taken together, was a stampede into what became known as "gentrification".

The first generation of children who had been brought up in Surrey and South London suburbia were less seduced by its pseudo-rural charms than their parents had been, and the commuter services provided by British Rail had deteriorated in comparison with what had earlier been offered by Southern. At the same time the effect of the Rent Act and local authority anxiety about tower blocks meant that there were run-down properties along the riverside going for a song. The in-thing became buying a house in Greenwich, Kennington, Camberwell, Stockwell, Clapham or Battersea, and doing it up. All these areas started to look a great deal smarter than they had done before, and gentrification generated welcome work for jobbing builders and created many other new forms of service employment. Opposition to the process was voiced in some of the Labour-run Borough Councils on behalf of the people who were supposed to be being displaced but, in the aftermath of Ronan Point, most of the Councils were happy to swim with the tide and to start implementing policies designed to encourage the doing-up of run-down properties. Other areas soon joined the list of desirable places in which to live, Nunhead, parts of Peckham and Brixton, Balham, Tooting and Wandsworth; a Brixton estate agent famously proclaimed that SW2 was at long last taking its rightful place alongside SW1 and SW3. And there was yet another example of the intentions of politicians being thwarted on the ground. Simultaneously with the gentrification of residential South London came the premiere appearance of the South London office block. In 1964, as well as bringing in the Rent Act, the Labour Government also imposed a ban on the building of new office space within London. The demand for new office space was, however, so strong, and so in excess of supply, that office rents rose to astronomic levels, and new offices started being created where there had been no offices before. This included south of the river, and office blocks mushroomed upwards at the southern ends of all the Thames bridges, from Tower Bridge to Chelsea, and also in places even further away, particularly in Croydon.

As well as losing their houses to eager and affluent incomers, the poorer people along the riverbank were also losing their jobs. The Wilson Government continued the policies of its Conservative predecessor in actively encouraging, with ever larger financial inducements, economic development outside London, and this development was inevitably at London's expense. The Government ingenuously justified its policies by declaring an intention to alleviate pressure on London's overloaded public services, but the effect was that industrial jobs along the South London riverbank declined drastically as companies relocated to the North and the Midlands, and as local employers found their overheads becoming prohibitive and went out of business. The Surrey Docks reached the end of their long and terminal decline, closing for good in 1970, and taking out with them a range of associated dockside industries. By the early 1970s London's manufacturing output had plummeted by 40% against pre-war levels, and industrial jobs along the South London riverbank by 75%; 70% of the jobs that London was left with were in the service sector, though the service sector by the definition used included solicitors and stockbrokers, as well as shelf-stackers in the new supermarkets which were increasingly displacing the traditional corner shops. Greater London's population, which had been 8.73 million in 1939, was half a million lower in 1970, and by 1980 had dropped by the same amount again. Most of this decline was a consequence of emigration to just the far side of the Green Belt, some of it to designated New Towns like Crawley, Basingstoke and Bracknell, but most of it to places in Kent, Surrey, Hampshire and Berkshire which were initially ill-equipped to cope with the influx. The overall effect on London, which could and should have been anticipated, was a serious brain drain, and the erosion of confidence and enterprise. Successive Labour Governments bemoaned the consequences of the policies for which they themselves had been largely responsible, and in 1976 Peter Shore, then Secretary of State for the Environment, described the South London riverbank as being left with "a disproportionate share of unskilled and semi-skilled workers, unemployment, one parent families, and overcrowded and inadequate housing". He might have added that Commonwealth immigrants, the newest arrivals and still the victims of racial prejudice, were being particularly hard hit. Inner South London was beginning to experience a new and unwelcome downwards spiral, trapping people in unsatisfactory circumstances which, at the same time, denied them any opportunity for escaping from them.

The Thatcher Years, 1979-1990

The woman who most profoundly affected the history of life in South London, seeing off all potential female rivals with little difficulty and with her customary disdain, was Margaret Hilda Thatcher. Her doctrine of consumerism, her implementation of the "right to buy", her setting up of the London Docklands Development Corporation, and her abolition of the GLC were all immensely influential, and were all in large measure attributable to her personally. And during her long tenure as Prime Minister she was almost personally responsible for the demise of South London's traditional working class, for the rise and fall of the "loony left", and for sowing the seeds of "New Labour". She believed passionately, in keeping with her Nonconformist upbringing, in personal freedom and personal responsibility and in the free play of market forces, and this, coupled with the increases in affluence which her policies managed to bring about, caused her famously to say "We are all middle class now". Less in keeping with her Nonconformist tradition was her equally famous declaration, "There is no such thing as society".

Myth has it that Margaret Thatcher won her elections by capturing the allegiance of Essex Man, but she also won over the hearts and minds of the men and women of Surrey and of South London's suburbia. Her policies were designed to give these people the freedom she assumed they craved for pursuing their own goals, uninhibited by the encumbrances of prohibitive taxation or intrusive bureaucratic control. And the size of her potential constituency was significantly increased as the consequences of her policies started to impinge. People whose jobs had been traditionally classified as "working class" became significantly better paid and started to think of themselves as potential Tories, the traditional authority of the Trade Unions and the movement's links with Labour were systematically eroded, and in particular the tenants of local authority housing were encouraged in exercising the right she had given them to purchase and own the homes that they lived in. The homes that were most enthusiastically purchased under the "Right to Buy" legislation were the earliest LCC estates of William Morris cottages, Eltham, Bellingham, St Helier and Roehampton, and the culture of these areas changed almost visibly and almost overnight. The same cultural changes also affected whole swathes of South London as people started working harder, and earning more money, and spending it headily on the things that they wanted to buy. But the Thatcher policies had their downside too. Driving a car was thought to imply a greater degree of consumer choice than catching a train; her encouragement of car ownership caused the roads to become congested, and railway commuting, for so long South London's mainstay, to become more and more of a nightmare as British Rail was progressively and deliberately starved of investment. The traditional demarcation between middle class affluence and working class poverty started to be replaced by a more pernicious systemic demarcation, the affluence of the "haves" and the poverty of the socially excluded. It very soon became clear that the new wealth being generated during the Thatcher era was failing to trickle all the way down.

The first evidence of the downside of Margaret Thatcher's policies was the rioting which devastated Brixton in April 1981. Lord Scarman was commissioned to inquire into what had happened and why, and in his subsequent report he placed most of the blame on decades of racial discrimination and the consequential exclusion of much of the black population from full participation in the life of the community (see page 33). A more precise defining moment in the changes she was bringing about, however, was the Bermondsey by-election later in the same year. The Bermondsey constituency had been represented in Parliament for many years by Bob Mellish, an embodiment of traditional Labour and a Minister in the Wilson and Callaghan Governments. In 1980 he announced his intention to retire, but the process of finding a successor for his apparently secure seat indicated that the Labour Party in Bermondsey was no longer the party of Morrison and Hayward. Morrison and Hayward had been very much "Old Labour", and their vision for their party was that it should represent the interests of the working man, and their assumption was that all working men had interests in common. They had gone in very little for consultation because they assumed that, as working men themselves, they understood instinctively what those interests were. They were Utopian in the sense that they assumed that the bosses were the enemy, that corporate ownership and corporate provision were the best means of bypassing the bosses, and that the Trade Unions were the vehicle through which these objectives would best be achieved. The Labour Party, in South London's poorer parts, had made a major contribution to working class solidarity since the twenties, and the Trade Unions had played an important social role. But times were changing, and the Labour Party found itself changing with them, losing its traditional working class membership and its traditional Trade Union base; it was no longer possible to think in terms of "working men" or of them having interests in common. Instead of nominating an Old Labour Trade Unionist, the Bermondsey Labour party instead nominated Peter Tatchell, the Branch Secretary and a local activist. Mellish was furious and disowned Tatchell, supporting instead John O'Grady, a local Southwark Councillor, who campaigned as a rival candidate under the banner of "Real Labour". Internecine warfare followed, with both O'Grady and Mellish making scarcely veiled snipes at Tatchell's declared homosexuality. Helped by this division of the Labour vote, the seat was won by the Liberal candidate Simon Hughes and, contrary to many people's expectations, Hughes has held the seat ever since. His tenure seems less surprising, however, when one remembers that Bermondsey had been a Liberal Party stronghold up till 1924.

The phenomenon of social activism had first become manifest in the field of local authority housing. All the riverside Boroughs had had policies of buying up land prior to the implementation of grandiose schemes of housing redevelopment, and large numbers of the houses which had been compulsorily purchased had been allowed to remain "disinhabited". At the same time, flats on the larger GLC estates, where the "Right to Buy" never managed to get off the ground, were becoming hard to let and even harder to live in, and there were also increasing numbers of people who were effectively homeless, many of them single parent families and recently arrived Commonwealth immigrants. Squatting campaigns were organised which were particularly successful in Lewisham and Lambeth, but which at the same time provoked considerable backlash; established residents who were dutifully paying their rents objected to the disruption caused by incomers who were paying nothing, and there was resentment against incomers, however needy, jumping the queue for the more viable local authority accommodation. South London's poor were becoming as various as they had been in the nineteenth century, and included mentally ill rough-sleepers, immigrants who spoke no English, and single mothers who were prevented from working by the paucity of child care. There was no Trade Union to represent the interests of these disparate groups, and they found themselves instead being led by activists, often of middle class origin and with their own personal axes to grind. Many of these activists had joined their local Labour Parties, and they persuaded their acolytes to do the same.

The battle lines within the Labour Party were drawn. In 1982 thirty-one of the Borough of Southwark's sixty-four Labour councillors were deselected, and eleven of them joined the then-flourishing Social Democratic Party which had broken away from Labour's right. Similar battles were fought in Lambeth where the Council was taken over by "Red" Ted Knight, and in the GLC. The Conservatives had captured the GLC in 1977 but lost it again in 1982, and the Labour Party that they lost it to was led by Ken Livingstone. The electoral arithmetic of Knight and Livingstone was simple. They reckoned that a quarter of the electorate was unemployed, black, feminist or gay, and that less than half the electorate was going to vote anyway so, in order to win, what they needed to do was court the minority vote. These minority voters were more interested in profiting from services designed for their benefit than they were in saving money on their rate bills, so Knight's Lambeth and Livingstone's GLC had little vested interest in constraining their expenditure. This was a shocking affront to Margaret Thatcher's deeply held principles. She was able to get rid of Ted Knight by surcharging the Lambeth Councillors and banning the most active of them from public office, but she had no powers at her disposal for ridding herself of Ken Livingstone. She therefore resorted to a solution of elegant simplicity, the abolition of the GLC.

The GLC had been established in 1964 only after a great deal of meticulous consideration and the deliberations of a Royal Commission. Twenty-one years later, however, it was abolished by the personal decision of one woman, a decision made in defiance of all moderate opinion including within her own Party. It was not just a matter of spite, though this probably entered into it; there was also the issue of GLC expenditure which was running out of control, and there was also a matter of political principle in that the main functions of the GLC were planning and intelligence, both of which Margaret Thatcher considered had become redundant since what mattered to her was the free play of market forces. So, after a banner had been hung from the County Hall balcony counting down the days that were left till its demise, and after a farewell party which trashed the Festival Hall, the GLC was formally abolished on 31 March 1986. But, even after its legal abolition, the GLC spent an unconscionable time a-dying. The London Residuary Body, established to tidy up its residual affairs, continued in existence for eight more years, spending a very long time relocating all the GLC staff, and an even longer time disposing of County Hall itself; the building was eventually sold to Sirayama, a provincial Japanese hotel company which notoriously held the Osaka franchise for MacDonald's. Some of the GLC's functions were carried on by the same staff operating as independent consultants, for example through the London Research Centre and the London Ecology Unit, with the latter selling its expertise as far away as China and Chile. Other GLC functions were taken over by the Government Office for London, and others by the City Corporation, and at the Seville International Exposition in 1992 London was officially represented by the London Docklands Development Corporation. But the absence of any sort of democratic authority in London did in fact matter, best exemplified, perhaps, by the fiasco of London's attempt to host the 2000 Olympic Games when two rival bids were put forward, one based on Wembley Stadium and the other on a new stadium to be built on the site of the Royal Docks; the two bids had the effect of cancelling each other out, and the Games were eventually held in Sydney which could hardly have been further away.

Margaret Thatcher was proud of her decision to abolish the GLC, and also proud of her decision to establish the London Docklands Development Corporation, but her pride in the latter was more widely shared. London had been an important port since Roman times, but its docks had long been a loss-making mess. Most of Europe's ports, during the sixteenth century, had opened up their waterfronts to become a visible and accessible part of the townscape, but London's riverside wharves remained invisible and inaccessible behind high brick walls of increasing grubbiness. An important opportunity for change was lost when the first inland docks were excavated in 1799, because of a decision to allow the Master Lightermen to retain their ancient "free-water privilege" of handling maritime cargoes without incurring dock dues or the costs of warehousing. This meant that a significant slice of the profit which the London docks should have been making was siphoned off into the pockets of the lightermen, and that there was no incentive to rationalise the string of small wharves which, with their associated small industries, continued to line the whole of the riverbank from Woolwich to Battersea. A heroic attempt to sort this situation out was made by Winston Churchill in 1909 when

How It Was Then, Greenland Dock 1953

he was Asquith's Liberal President of the Board of Trade; he established the Port of London Authority to manage all the docks as a single entity, including Tilbury with its potential as a major deep-water port. But even this scheme didn't work, because all the profits that accrued as Tilbury was developed were used to subsidise inefficient and loss-making activity everywhere else. Daily hiring didn't end in London till 1966 when the London docks were starting to close, and when the Dock Labour Scheme was introduced as yet another sop to Union pressure; existing dockers started getting paid even when, which happened increasingly often, there was not even the prospect of work, and their sick pay and superannuation inexorably increased as they all became inexorably older. The Scheme was eventually abolished in 1989, and at long last Tilbury was liberated from its obligation to subsidise the docks upstream so that it could start to become profitable.

The Surrey Docks closed for good in 1970, and for the next decade the political parties squabbled over what to do with the land that had been released. Labour, whenever in power at Westminster or at County Hall, wanted the docklands developed as sites for light industry in order to create jobs for the dockers and others who were being put out

25

of work, while the Conservatives, whenever and wherever they were in power, wanted the riverside developed as upmarket housing and marinas for expensive yachts. This bickering resulted in stalemate, and the Surreys were alternately filled in and then re-excavated. This infuriated Margaret Thatcher and in 1980, only a year after becoming Prime Minister, she set up the London Docklands Development Corporation. The LDDC was given a totally free hand for developing the docklands, unencumbered by any planning considerations which might have been imposed by Government, by the GLC, or by the riverside Boroughs. A building spree resulted which, in the almost total absence of any master plan or architectural guidelines, might have been an aesthetic disaster, but the result has been described as the jewel in Margaret Thatcher's crown. On the north bank it resulted in the elegant pinnacle of Canary Wharf and a significant shift in London's centre of gravity, perhaps the first for a thousand years, from west to east, and on the south bank it resulted in the development of the Surreys, not as the Surrey Docks but as the better sounding Surrey Quays. The riverside warehouses were converted into expensive flats and, where there weren't warehouses, expensive blocks of flats were erected with ex-warehouse facades which resembled them. The LDDC did in fact make two valuable planning contributions, the Thames Path which the developers of riverside sites were required to create, and the sculpture which was commissioned along its way.

Where We Are Now, 1990-2005

Margaret Thatcher resigned as Prime Minister in 1990 and was succeeded by John Major, the only Prime Minister so far to have been born and educated within the Diocese of Southwark. He surprised everybody except himself by winning the General Election of 1992, and during his period in office the Labour Party spent much of the time reinventing itself as "New Labour", stealing in the process a number of Margaret Thatcher's discarded clothes. Labour won back power in 1997, and the manifesto for its successful General Election campaign included a commitment to provide a "Voice for London", a commitment which was honoured in 2001 when elections were held for the new post of London's Mayor. The winner, following a somewhat similar change of clothes, was Ken Livingstone; he had riled Tony Blair almost as much as he had riled Margaret Thatcher, and Blair had carefully arranged his non-selection as Labour's candidate, but Livingstone nonetheless scored an overwhelming victory on an independent ticket. Manifestations of his mayoralty south of the river so far have included the Congestion Charge Zone, a fleet of new environmentally-correct buses some of which bend in the middle, and his new riverside office block just upstream from Tower Bridge, designed by Sir Norman Foster and looking like a large skewed egg. Other new arrivals on the riverbank have been the Globe Theatre, opened in 1997, the new Tate Modern, opened in 2000, and a number of other projects planned to celebrate the Millennium including the footbridge from Tate Modern to St Paul's whose opening had to be postponed because of wobble, the giant bicycle wheel of the London Eye and, of course, the Millennium Dome. Along with the Dome came the extension of the Jubilee Line which was built to service it, the first addition to the Underground since the Victoria Line extension to Brixton opened in 1971; the Docklands Light Railway, begun in 1979 and technically not a part of the Underground, had crossed the river en route for Lewisham in 1999.

A fitting note on which to end this brief survey of South London's history during the twentieth century is to ask questions about the Millennium Dome. Its site on the Greenwich peninsular had the advantage of straddling the meridian, but the disadvantage of having been so comprehensively polluted by earlier industrial misuse that it had effectively been abandoned. Most of the project's much-publicised financial overspend went on cleaning up the top-soil and providing amenities like electricity, water and roads, and in particular the North Greenwich tube station which reconnected the area to main-stream civilisation. Four thousand local people were trained and employed, and the chaplaincy team which served it was truly ecumenical, the first occasion on which the London City Mission has worked with Roman Catholics. The Dome itself was a highly complex and innovative construction which was brought in on time, and the exhibition which it housed was visited by more people during 2000 than any other public attraction despite it being the first "experience" predicated on discouraging access by car. And the people who visited it gave it a 90% approval rating. But what is interesting is the way that it has come to be thought of, almost universally, as a failure, including by people who visited it and enjoyed it and went back for more. One way of answering this conundrum is to point to the negative publicity which was generated as a consequence of the significant journalists who attended its opening being made to spend too long standing in a queue, but there is perhaps a more intriguing possibility. Perhaps the exhibition was in fact a great success, and perhaps its successfulness lay in the unsettling effect that it had upon the people who went to it and said they enjoyed it. Perhaps we live in unsettled times, and the Millennium Experience, albeit unconsciously, managed to get it right. The Great Exhibition of 1851 celebrated the triumphs of technology, and it looked forward, with exhilaration and some justification, to the resolution of the nineteenth century's seemingly intractable problems through technology's pragmatic application. The Festival of Britain in 1951 looked nostalgically backwards to what Britain had represented in the days when it had been Great, and enabled people to feel better than they would otherwise have done by offering them the illusion that the Greatness was going shortly to be restored. But how might the Millennium have best been celebrated? Without a doubt the standard of living in South London is immeasurably higher than it was in 1851 or in 1951, and there is every probability that in the future it will get better still, and this, surely, is a cause for celebration. So why do we feel so unsettled? Perhaps it is because the factors which are bringing about the present beneficial changes are so intangible. Everything that was on display at the Crystal Palace in 1851, from railway locomotives to sewing machines, was nothing if not tangible; as one commentator put it at the time, "you can hit it with a hammer". But you can't hit with a hammer a direct debit, an e-mail, or a web-site. Nevertheless, virtual reality is no less real for being virtual, even though it may not make for an exhilarating exhibition. Perhaps our unsettledness has something to do with values. Everything that was on display at the Festival of Britain embodied values, albeit values nostaligically hankered after because they were already in the process of erosion. But we still have values, even if they are more pluralist and less clearly articulated because supported by a less obvious consensus. Measuring progress is difficult when there is no agreement as to the criteria against which progress should be measured, but the value of looking back over a hundred years of South London's history is that the progress that has been made becomes that much easier to appreciate. Within the framework of a century-long continuum the contrasts become starker, the changes more obvious, and the prospect of the future, whatever uncertainties it may hold, that much less intimidating.

SECTION TWO:
ASPECTS OF LIFE IN SOUTH LONDON
Immigration and Race

There were black people in England before there were English; an inscription found at Burgh-on-Sands in Cumbria indicates that amongst the troops defending Hadrian's Wall in the second century, three hundred years before the Anglo-Saxon invasions, was a division of "Moors raised and trained in Africa". And recorded instances of xenophobic discrimination against black people go back at least as far as 1596 when Queen Elizabeth I wrote to the Lord Mayor of London, "Her Majestie understanding that there are of late divers blackmoors brought into this Realme, of which kinde of people there are already here too manie, Her Majestie's pleasure therefore ys that these kinde of people be sent forth from the lande". Further evidence that black people were a common enough sight on London's streets during the sixteenth century is the sheer quantity of references to them in Elizabethan drama. It was during the late seventeenth century, however, that their numbers increased significantly; they arrived as merchants, sailors and servants, and Pepys employed a cook whom he glowingly described as "a blackmoor who dresses our meat mighty well, and we mightily pleased with her".

The middle of the eighteenth century was the heyday of the three-passage slave trade when manufactured goods were shipped from England to Africa, slaves from Africa to the colonies in America and the West Indies, and cotton and sugar from America and the West Indies back to England. Bristol and then Liverpool are usually thought of as the main slave ports, but in fact London did more business than either, and many rich merchants brought their domestic slaves back with them as servants. In 1772 Lord Chief Justice Mansfield, in a celebrated court case concerning a slave called James Somerset who had refused to return with his master to Jamaica, determined that slave status had no standing in English law, and black Londoners threw a party in a tavern in Southwark to drink the Lord Chief Justice's health. There are records of racist attitudes in the eighteenth century, but they are used to justify the institution of slavery rather than the persecution of black individuals. Alexander Knox, Provost-Marshal of the Colony of Georgia, wrote in 1757, "Whether the Creator originally formed these black people a little lower than other men, or that they have lost their intellectual powers through disease, I will not assume the province of determining, but certain it is that the negro is a complete definition of indolent stupidity", and he went on to oppose the education of slaves on the grounds that it rendered them less suitable for work. The opposite view was advanced by the growing lobby of campaigners for the abolition of slavery who stressed the equality of all people in the sight of God; during the eighteenth century this movement was spearheaded by John Wesley and the early Methodists, but in the first years of the nineteenth the leadership passed to an Evangelical group within the Church of England, based in South London and known as the Clapham Sect, of which the most prominent member was William Wilberforce.

By the middle of the nineteenth century both the slave trade and slavery had been statutorily abolished within the British Empire, but racial prejudice had by no means disappeared. Two remarkable black people made public appearances on Kennington Common, in 1848 and 1857 respectively, though in very different circumstances. The first was William Cuffay, born in Chatham in 1788 and the son of a freed slave who had got a job as a cook on a warship. He worked as a tailor, joined the Owenite National Consolidated Trades Union, came out on strike as part of a campaign for better working conditions, and thereafter found it impossible to get work. He became a leader in the Chartist movement, and in 1848 assembled on Kennington Common the largest of the Chartist rallies; fashionable London held its breath, the Commissioner of Police declared the gathering illegal, tens of thousands of shopkeepers and clerks were enrolled as special constables, and Queen Victoria was dispatched to the assumed safety of the Isle of Wight. But, inhibited by the glowering presence of the special constables and by torrential rain, the Chartists decided not to march. Cuffay was arrested, tried, and convicted on the evidence of two police spies. "He is a nigger", sneered The Times, "and some of the others are Irish. We doubt if there are half a dozen Englishmen in the whole lot". He was sentenced to transportation for life but soon, because of his exemplary behaviour, started working for wages as a tailor in Hobart, was pardoned in 1856 but chose not to come home, and died in 1870 at the age of eighty-two.

The second was Mary Seacole who was born in Jamaica in 1805, the daughter of a Scottish soldier and an ex-slave practitioner of traditional medicine. Mary had "a yearning for medical knowledge and practice", and in due course began caring for British Army officers as "a nurse and doctress". In 1851, at the height of the California goldrush, she set up a house in Panama where she looked after cholera victims, and one white American whom she had cured attempted to flatter her, when proposing her health, by suggesting that she bleach her skin to make her "as acceptable as she deserves to be". She responded by saying "I do not appreciate your kind wishes with respect to my complexion; had I been as dark as any nigger I should have been just as happy and as useful, but I nonetheless drink to you too, and to the general reformation of American manners". She came to London in 1854 and, learning of the collapse of the British Army's nursing arrangements in the Crimean War, applied to the War Office to be sent out to help. She was turned down, including personally by Florence Nightingale and by Sidney Herbert, the Secretary of State for War, despite all the glowing testimonials she was able to produce from officers serving in the Crimea whom she had earlier nursed in the West Indies. Her reaction was to assemble a comprehensive stock of medicines and home comforts, purchase her own boat ticket, and sail off to Balaclava. There she served tea on the landing stages, and set up "The British Hotel" where she cared for scores of demoralised and wounded soldiers of all ranks who brought home stories of her compassion and sense of humour, and of her fearlessness under fire; she said that she had no difficulty in throwing herself to the ground when being fired upon, but great difficulty in getting up again because of the stoutness of her physique. She became a nationally known figure as a consequence of the eulogistic reports about her which were filed by W.H.Russell, the war correspondent of The Times. At the end of the war she was bankrupt and in debt, but she received no official compensation. Such was the gratitude of the Crimean veterans, however, that a benefit was arranged for her on Kennington Common. Sitting in state between two Generals, Lord Rokeby and Lord George Paget, she watched a thousand performers and listened to nine military bands, and this cleared her debts so that when she died in 1881 she was able to bequeath £2,500, a considerable sum at the time. In a television poll in 2004 she was voted "Top Black Briton".

The myth of black inferiority, used during the eighteenth century to justify slavery, was used in the second half of the nineteenth to justify Empire. Given that the British ruled a third of the world's population, being British had to mean being best. Rudyard Kipling in "The White Man's Burden" described other races as "lesser breeds" and as "half savage and half child", and more surprisingly the classicist and liberal humanitarian Gilbert Murray wrote in 1900, without a trace of irony, "There is in the world a hierarchy of races. Those nations which eat more, claim more, and get higher wages will direct and rule others, and the lower work of the world will tend to be done by the lower breeds of men. This much we of the ruling colour accept as obvious". Charles Darwin demonstrated that all people, black and white alike, were equally descended from apes, but his hypothesis of the "Survival of the Fittest" was distorted to support a doctrine known as "Social Darwinism" which proclaimed that, since white people were demonstrably fitter than black people, they were therefore destined to survive at all other races' expense. There is, however, little recorded evidence of black people being actively persecuted in England during the nineteenth century, probably because such black people as there were were subsumed within the general mass of the nation's poor, where they had as hard a time of it as everybody else.

During the First World War significant numbers of black Empire troops were posted to Europe, notably from India, West Africa and the West Indies and, though they encountered very little trouble while they were fighting in France, they were subjected to violent racial attacks when they returned to England prior to being demobilised; the worst of the violence happened in Cardiff and on Tyneside, but there were also some nasty incidents in London. Between the wars, three remarkable black men were active in South London. One was Dr Harold Moody, born in Jamaica in 1882, who came to study medicine at King's College Hospital, where he won prizes and qualified as a doctor in 1910. He was denied a hospital appointment because the Matron "refused to have a coloured doctor working on the wards" and then, despite being the best qualified candidate, was rejected for the post of Medical Officer for the Camberwell Board of Guardians. He set himself up as a General Practitioner in Peckham, and in 1931 established the League of Coloured Peoples with the stated aim of "improving relations between the races". Moody was committed to moderation and negotiation, and through the League he achieved a great deal; he protested to the BBC about their use of the word "nigger" and received a letter of abject apology from Lord Reith and a promise never to do it again, but his greatest achievement was the banning of discrimination on grounds of colour throughout the British armed forces. There was remarkably little racial trouble during the Second World War, and Moody deserves much of the credit; all five of his children, two of them daughters, served as commissioned officers. Much more radical than Moody were John Archer and Shapurji Saklatvala, who between them became Britain's first elected black councillor, Britain's first black Mayor, and Britain's first black MP. Archer was born in Liverpool in 1863 and moved to South London in 1890; he was elected to Battersea Borough Council in 1906, became Mayor in 1913, and continued to serve on the Council with distinction till the late 1930s. Saklatvala, a Parsee from Bombay (Mumbai), was elected with Archer's support as Labour MP for Battersea North in 1922, but lost the seat the following year only to be re-elected in 1924, though as a member of the Communist Party. His re-election was significantly helped by Archer having ensured that there was no Labour opposition, and to date he is the Diocese of Southwark's only black and only Communist MP. By strange coincidence and in high irony, he was cremated at Golders Green on the same afternoon as Rudyard Kipling.

Such racial trouble as there was in World War II resulted from the arrival of the Americans. Unlike the British army, the American army was still segregated into separate black and white units, and white American soldiers objected violently to sharing restaurants and dance-halls with black British troops. The worst violence happened in Liverpool but

Great Expectations, Brixton 1965

there was also trouble in South London, though the records there suggest that the white British troops, to their credit, weighed in alongside their black compatriots. At the end of the war there was a serious labour shortage, and a serious shortage of housing. Throughout much of the Empire, however, there was chronic unemployment and no social security provision, and Empire veterans returned to their home countries with their social expectations significantly raised by their war experience to find there was no work for them, and no social role. Emigration back to Britain was an obvious aspiration (see page 17), and the Empire Windrush with its cargo of immigrants from the Caribbean docked in Tilbury on 22 June 1948, soon to be followed by trickles of immigrants from India, from Pakistan, from Cyprus, and from all the British colonies in the West Indies. A number of British employers launched systematic campaigns to recruit West Indian labour, including London Transport and the National Health Service, and Enoch Powell when Minister for Health went out of his way to welcome West Indian nurses. The immigrants arrived with a strong motivation to find work and, having learned to read from text books which extolled the mother country's virtues, with high expectations of a warm welcome. But what they actually encountered was very different. The new arrivals found themselves being discriminated against in housing, notoriously encountering "Whites Only" signs in boarding houses, and in employment, where white Trade Unionists frequently went on strike in protest against having to work alongside them. Even though more than half of Britain's population had never met anybody who was black, over two thirds admitted to being racially prejudiced and to holding assumptions that black people were "primitive, uncivilised, and over-sexed". "People talk about a colour problem arising in Britain, but how can there be a colour problem?", asked the

Labour MP Tom Driberg in 1952. "Even after all the immigration of the past few years, there are only 190,000 coloured people in our population, four out of every thousand. The real problem is not black skins but white prejudice. It is prejudice, and the surrender to prejudice, that we have to fight".

This prejudice was bound, sooner or later, to be expressed in action, and racist riots broke out in August 1958, first in Nottingham and then in Notting Hill, where publicity given to fairly innocuous incidents drew in young white men who were looking for an opportunity for "nigger-bashing". The riots were roundly condemned by the liberal establishment, but the racist tail quickly began to wag the liberal dog. A Commonwealth Immigrants Bill was published, blatantly pandering to racist attitudes by proposing that Commonwealth citizens be deprived of their British passports and that the immigration of black people be restricted by right of entry being made dependant on a voucher system. But this notice of intent proved massively counter-effective. Prior to the Bill's eventual enactment in 1962, the trickle of immigrants expanded into a torrent, and tens of thousands of people set out from all over the world in a desperate effort to "beat the ban". Indian and Pakistani arrivals jumped from 3,000 in 1959 to 48,000 in 1961, West Indian arrivals from 16,000 to 66,000, and Cypriot immigration quadrupled. As earlier immigrants had before them, the newcomers tended to go to areas where their known compatriots had already settled; Jamaicans went to Brixton and Greek Cypriots went to Peckham, while Indians and Pakistanis for the most part settled north of the river.

Labour opposed the Commonwealth Immigrants Bill and then won the 1964 General Election, an election that was marred by racism, most notoriously by Peter Griffiths' slogan in Smethwick, "if you want a nigger neighbour, vote Labour". The Labour Government immediately sought to ameliorate the situation by passing the Race Relations Act of 1965 which made discrimination on grounds of race illegal, and by establishing the Race Relations Board to oversee the Act's implementation. But Labour too continued to implement racist policies, in particular the Commonwealth Immigrants Act of 1968 which restricted the right of entry of Asians from Kenya, and later Uganda, whilst allowing in Commonwealth immigrants who were white by virtue of their "patriality"; James Callaghan as Home Secretary justified the measure on grounds of its popular acceptability. Then, in April 1968 at a rally in Birmingham, Enoch Powell made his "rivers of blood" speech. He predicted that, in twenty to thirty years time, the population of Inner London "would be, at the absolute theoretical minimum, one third to one half coloured". Edward Heath, to his credit, promptly sacked him from the Shadow cabinet, but Powell became a hero overnight and the National Front started to organise racist marches. The 1970s were a time of high unemployment, and unemployment hit black people much harder than whites. There was trouble too in schools, both from National Front sympathisers who didn't want their children educated alongside blacks, and also from well-meaning liberal teachers who failed their black pupils by assuming low expectations on their behalf. But the greatest difficulty by far was discrimination by the police and by the courts. The police constantly refused to protect black communities which came under attack from white aggressors, and implemented heavy-handed reprisals in response to black people's efforts at self-defence. White perpetrators were seldom arrested and, on the occasions when they were brought to court, were often acquitted or given derisorily small sentences because of the tendency of the courts to accept the evidence of the police rather than of the victims. The worst case in South London was in January 1981 when an unprovoked arson attack on a house in Deptford killed thirteen black youngsters. The police discounted the possibility that the killings

32

had been racially motivated and immediately used this as a pretext for failing to make any arrests, and two months later fifteen thousand people, mainly but not entirely black, marched in protest the ten miles from Deptford to Westminster to demand remedial action. A grossly belated inquiry into the incident was announced in 2004.

Something had to blow, and blow it did. In April 1980 there were riots in the St Paul's area of Bristol, and a year later, two months after the Deptford arson attack, there were riots in Brixton and then in Toxteth in Liverpool. These were followed by riots in a number of smaller places, including some as unlikely as Windsor. There is an inherent irony in that the three most serious riots of the early 1980s happened in the eighteenth century's three major slave ports. The riots in Brixton were a consequence of Operation Swamp, a heavy-handed crackdown on street crime organised by the Metropolitan Police. As in most places, the trouble was triggered by a comparatively trivial occurrence which provoked a police over-reaction; a young man was arrested on Wiltshire Road, the crowd then attempted to release him, and the police weighed in. For two nights the streets of Brixton became a battle ground as both black and white youths fought the police in an orgy of vandalism, looting and arson; over two hundred people were arrested and over two hundred policemen hurt. Commissioner Sir David McNee defended Operation Swamp by saying that the high level of street crime demanded a strong police presence, but community leaders insisted that the riots were a consequence of decades of discriminatory policing.

An important consequence of the Brixton riots was the setting up of a Commission of Inquiry conducted by Lord Scarman, who skillfully endeared himself to the black population and was addressed throughout as "Lord" as though it was his Christian name. His report identified the causes of the riots as being the cumulation of three decades of discrimination which had resulted in poor housing and reduced employment opportunities, racial harassment, biased policing, and a consequential alienation of the black population from the mainstream culture. The Thatcher Government responded with minimal sympathy and Norman Tebbitt, Secretary of State for Employment, when told that youth unemployment had been a contributory cause, famously declared, "my father didn't riot, he got on his bike and looked for work". But from then on things did start to get a great deal better. The culture was beginning to change; a whole generation of white South Londoners had grown up with black neighbours whom they had got to know personally, and the ethos established by the Race Relations Board was beginning to permeate thinking and practice. Scarman deserves some of the credit for having accurately charted a course for future improvements, but Margaret Thatcher, despite the contempt that she showed for his report, deserves more of it because she set the national economy on course for a long and sustainable economic boom. The boom benefited most people in South London, but it benefited black people disproportionately, and black people became better able than ever before, by their own efforts, to buy their own houses and to establish themselves on career patterns of their own choosing. Of course, not all people were able to benefit. The shadow side of the Thatcher boom was the "social exclusion" of those who, for whatever reason, got left behind, and the socially excluded included a share of people who were black. Xenophobia did not disappear, but it started being focused on illegal immigrants and asylum seekers rather than on the ethnic minorities already here.

The one issue which remained untackled throughout the eighties was racism within the police. Then, on 22 April 1993, a black teenager called Stephen Lawrence was stabbed to death at a bus stop in Eltham. His alleged killers were brought to court, but the conviction failed and accusations were made of police bungling. The Lawrence family then brought in a private prosecution which also failed, and later demanded that the Government set up an inquiry into the handling of the case. The Conservative Government refused, but in 1997 Jack Straw, the incoming Labour Home Secretary, set one up under the chairmanship of Sir William Macpherson. The most important phrase in the eventual Macpherson Report was "institutional racism". The Metropolitan Police were shamed into putting their house in order, and this to a creditable extent they managed to do under the leadership of a new Commissioner, Sir Paul Condon. And at the same time all other institutions, including the Church of England, were encouraged to examine their own procedures and assumptions to see whether they too were guilty of institutional racism, and if so to take the necessary remedial action. Three years later, on 27 November 2000, another black youngster was murdered within the diocese, Damilola Taylor; but in his case there was little accusation of institutional racism, and the emphasis was on the unsatisfactory living conditions on the North Peckham Estate.

There is no record in the Southwark Diocesan archive of the Church in South London having taken any significant action on racial issues prior to the episcopacy of Mervyn Stockwood. This inaction is not altogether surprising, since race relations was never a national issue during the first half of the century, and the black population, both nationally and within the diocese, was comparatively small. Stockwood was mindful of the needs of black people in his campaign to rejuvenate the poor parishes along the South London riverbank, and on several occasions in the House of Lords he spoke out on racial issues, most notably in opposing the 1962 Commonwealth Immigrants Act. He appointed a Chichester-ordained Indian, Ivor Smith Cameron, as Diocesan Missioner, and it is worth noting in passing that in 1965 a young black South African was appointed curate in Bletchingley in rural Surrey; his name was Desmond Tutu. The first truly proactive Southwark Bishop in the field of race relations was David Sheppard when Bishop of Woolwich between 1969 to 1975 (see page 92). He made a significant gesture in refusing to live in his predecessor's house in Blackheath, and moved instead to Asylum Road in Peckham, a street where the majority of residents were black. Many of the newly arrived Commonwealth immigrants, particularly those from the West Indies, had been committed churchgoers back home, and they came to worship in Anglican churches in South London assuming that they would be welcomed. Given that two thirds of the British population at that time admitted to racial prejudice, it would have been unrealistic to expect church congregations to have been drawn solely from the unprejudiced residue, and several early black worshippers found themselves being shunned by white members of their congregations who would move away from them to sit in a different pew. The understandable reaction of many black Christians was to transfer to a different church, and a number of specifically black Pentecostalist churches were established in South London during the seventies, some of them in superfluous buildings which the Church of England had vacated. Sheppard was very aware of all this, and he launched a number of initiatives designed to make black people feel more welcome and to ensure their better integration into the Church's structures. He set up a Diocesan Race Relations Group within the Council for Social Aid whose membership included Canon Mick Pinder, Revd Bob Nind and Revd Jack Pawsey, an NSM attached to St George's Camberwell; Horace Parkinson, a black youngster from Brixton, was employed as a case worker. Sheppard also recruited into the diocese Wilfred Wood, born in Barbados and ordained at St Paul's, as Vicar of St Lawrence Catford.

Sheppard was succeeded as Bishop of Woolwich by Michael Marshall. During the early eighties the National Front was particularly active in South London, and its leader was a resident of Lewisham called Martin Webster. Marshall confronted Webster on radio and on television on several occasions and, alongside Stockwood and Lewisham's Mayor, led a protest march against the Front's activities. The Southwark Diocesan Synod passed a strong motion proposed by Hugh Montefiore, then Bishop of Kingston, affirming the worth and rights of black people in Britain, and in 1983 Bishop Keith Sutton, Montefiore's successor, piloted through Synod a motion which established the Southwark Diocese Race Relations Commission, the first such initiative in any English diocese; David Udo, a Brixton school teacher born in Nigeria, was appointed its first director. The publication of "Faith in the City" in 1982 had stimulated a number of important race relations initiatives, particularly through the designation and special funding of Urban Priority Areas (see page 95). A black member of the Archbishops' Commission which produced the report, Barry Thorley, was appointed Vicar of St Matthew's Brixton, and in April 1985 Wilfred Wood was appointed Bishop of Croydon, the first black Bishop in England (see page 95). Interestingly, his appointment was announced during the same week that, north of the river, Bernie Grant was elected the country's first Afro-Caribbean MP. In 1992, in the aftermath of a debate in Diocesan Synod, Bishop Peter Selby, who had succeeded Sutton, established the diocese's Black and Minority Ethnic Forum, which continues in business, arranging annual conferences and identifying areas where initiative is called for. The Forum's declared aim is to provide "opportunities for the voices and views of black and minority ethnic members of the Church throughout Southwark Diocese to be freely expressed on any matter of concern, interest and importance to them, and to enable them to articulate their perceptions, affirm their worship, faith and culture as active members of the family of God". In 1999, following the publication of the Macpherson Report, Diocesan Synod set up an independent inquiry into institutional racism within the structures of the Diocese of Southwark itself; the inquiry's report made specific recommendations which aimed to increase black representation on electoral rolls, on PCCs, and on Deanery Synods, and to increase the numbers of black clergy. It also recommended training in racial awareness for key diocesan staff, including the four bishops. Bishop Tom Butler deserves credit for championing this inquiry and for his determined implementation of its recommendations, and the diocese now has a black Archdeacon in Daniel Kajumba of Reigate.

South London has always been a haven for immigrants, and is now home for a larger number than at any previous time. Today's immigrants are almost certainly more diverse than ever before, and almost certainly they now represent the highest ever proportion of the population. There are sizable communities of Vietnamese in Lewisham and of Portuguese in Vauxhall, the Indian community in Tooting is the second largest in London after Southall, the biggest concentration of Koreans outside Seoul is in New Malden and the diocese is now funding its first Korean worker, there is a French *Lycee* in Clapham, there are twenty-five thousand South Africans in Wandsworth and a number of Anglican services are now held in Afrikaans, and clergy in the Wandsworth Archdeaconry alone come from Jamaica, Nigeria, Australia, Germany, the United States, France, Belgium, Poland and Peru.

Employment

There is a celebrated picture by Monet, painted by happy coincidence in the year in which the Diocese of Southwark was founded, of Waterloo Bridge looking south. Downstream of the bridge he shows a forest of factory chimneys belching smoke and, though in his skilled impressionist hands the smoke is made to look beautiful, it must have been less than pleasant for the people who had to live and work in its midst. What this picture makes clear is that, in 1905, the south bank of the Thames was still a major manufacturing centre, in direct continuity with the "stink industries" of the seventeenth century. Monet's factories, together with the Surrey Docks a little further downstream, provided plenty of employment, but this employment was never very secure. Much of the work was seasonal, especially in the food processing industries, and poor people were constantly migrating into the area which in consequence kept wage rates low. The "hiring at the gate" system for employing dockers was particularly notorious. A series of strikes in 1911 led to the formation of the Transport and General Workers Union for the dockers and the Railwaymen's Union for the employees of the various railway companies, but brought few immediate advantages; South London was not fertile ground for Trade Unionism, and widespread Union membership did not get established till after the First World War. A great many of South London's manual workers remained un-Unionised because the factories and workshops of their employers were so small, and there were always people along the riverbank who had no regular work at all.

The Stink Industries, Great Dover Street c 1905

Not all the earliest residents of the Diocese of Southwark, however, were so unfortunate. The most secure employment was provided by the Armed Services; there were the soldiers of the Royal Artillery and the Royal Engineers in Woolwich, and the civilians employed in the Royal Arsenal and in its neighbouring munitions factories, and in the naval dockyard in Deptford which remained operational till 1918. And, commuting into the City from the semicircle of railway suburbs, there were the legions of clerks. It is difficult for us nowadays to envisage the type of employment implied by being an Edwardian clerk. In the days before word-processors, photocopiers and even typewriters, all official documents had to be written out in longhand, and at the bottom of the profession were the copy clerks who made copies of letters and documents for the files. Above them were junior administrators who composed letters and directives in line with existing policies, and who kept the accounts. And the term "clerk" also embraced quite senior administrators who determined and implemented policy; the Civil Service grade of Principal is an abbreviation of Principal Clerk. All these clerks were seriously middle class, respectable and respectful, mindful of the necessity of keeping up appearances, and for the most part stalwart members of the Church of England.

Prior to the Second World War the Church of England had little interaction with the world of paid employment. Conscientious suburban vicars confined themselves to taking Sunday services, to hatchings matchings and dispatchings, and to visiting members of their congregations in their homes. Along the riverbank people in work tended to be Methodists or, if they were Irish, Roman Catholics. The scores of deconsecrated Nonconformist chapels, now used for storage or as workshops or even as homes, bear testimony to this, as does the decision, implemented in 1850, to found the Roman Catholic Diocese of Southwark and to build for it a new cathedral (see page 74). The main focus of Church of England mission work along the riverbank, including that based in the College and Public School settlements which had been founded in the closing years of Queen Victoria's reign, was helping the families where there was no breadwinner or no breadwinner in work, and a major concern of the parishes was keeping going the C of E denominational schools.

Trade Unionism came into its own in South London in the aftermath of World War I. The deal which Lloyd George, then Minister of Munitions, had done with the Trade Unions in 1915 which suspended their privileges for the duration of the war, had had little impact within the diocese because very few privileges had been negotiated, though it had had the temporary effect of bringing large numbers of women into the labour force for the first time. After the war, however, when unemployment became widespread, Trade Unionism came into its own. The Trade Unions negotiated secure conditions for their members and kept wage rates artificially high, and workers had a strong vested interest in maintaining their Union membership. The people who suffered were the unemployed, and the acquisition of a Union card became a longed-for aspiration. During the 1930s the economy started to pick up again as South London regained some of its eminence as a manufacturing centre, and unemployment became less widespread. And then, almost immediately after the declaration of World War II, unemployment disappeared altogether; the demand for men in the armed services, coupled with the increased economic activity that was needed to sustain the war effort, created a significant labour shortage, and women were once again called upon to go out to work.

Curiously, perhaps because there were no longer unemployed people who might have been thought of as deserving pastoral priority, it was at this point that the Church of England first started to involve itself in the world of work. The pioneers within the Diocese of Southwark were Cuthbert Bardsley and Colin Cuttell. Bardsley had worked with the legendary Tubby Clayton at Toc H, and in 1940 was appointed Vicar of Woolwich. He arrived there to discover that the area was regularly being bombed, that his church windows had been blown out and replaced with hardboard, and that his congregation had dwindled almost to nil. During the air raids he often found himself sharing a shelter with the employees of Siemens, ironically then a German firm but later to become AEI (Associated Electrical Industries), and he started using this enforced incarceration as an opportunity for talking about God. This soon led to him being invited back to the factory, and there he started taking services using as a model the Toc H liturgy which he had developed with Clayton. In 1944 he was appointed Provost of Southwark Cathedral, and he recruited Cuttell, a young priest from Canada, to exercise a "ministry without portfolio", though his portfolio included continuing and expanding the link with Siemens. Cuttell also developed similar links with other employers in the Woolwich area, forming in the process good working relationships with a number of local Trade Unionists including Arthur Deakin, Vic Feather and Jack Jones. Bardsley, meanwhile, continued the same sort of work in the neighbourhood of the cathedral, and he instituted the Tuesday Fellowship which met weekly in the Harvard Chapel, and an annual "Industrial Harvest Festival". Strong links were formed with Guy's Hospital, and with Hibernia Wharf whose Chairman Sir Rupert de la Bere was later to become both Lord Mayor of London and Chairman of the South London Industrial Mission.

Almost in passing a new sort of theology began to develop, based around the perceived need for being "alongside" people in the situations where "alongsideness" actually mattered, and around sharing in people's work lives and in the work issues which were concerning them. This theology owed a great deal to Tubby Clayton's book "Fishers of Men", and also to work being done in the Roman Catholic Church in France. Shortly before the Second World War, in order to demonstrate their solidarity with the socially excluded and the "unchurched", French *pretres-ouvriers* had begun taking manual jobs in factories and in the badly paid service industries. During the war a number of them went "underground", ministering to their compatriots without making their priesthood overt, and some even allowed themselves to be transported, voluntarily and *incognito*, as slave labour to the concentration camps in Germany. This sort of activity continued after the war under the banner of the *Mission de France*, and it was actively encouraged by Cardinal Suhart, then the Archbishop of Paris, who famously declared, when attempting to fend off the criticism that the value of this mission was impossible to quantify, "the first fifty years are going to be the hardest". In 1953 the *Mission de France* was summarily axed by the Vatican on the grounds that *pretres-ouvriers* were becoming contaminated by association with the Communist CGT.

In 1946 Bardsley left Southwark Cathedral to become Bishop of Croydon, then in the Diocese of Canterbury, and was replaced as Provost by Hugh Ashdown, who continued to support Cuttell in his industrial work. Bardsley later became Bishop of Coventry, and Ashdown Bishop of Newcastle. The years that followed World War II were a time of chronic labour shortage both nationally and in South London, and the general assumption was that the spectre of unemployment had once and finally been laid to rest; the area's industrial base remained secure, and the setting up of the Welfare State was creating additional jobs within the public sector. A number of employers started asking themselves what they might best do to attract and retain workers and, at the same time, a number of employment practices started attracting adverse criticism. This phenomenon increased during the late 1950s when a number of London employers, in particular London Transport and the National Health Service, embarked upon recruitment campaigns in the West Indies and elsewhere. As a consequence of the work already done by Bardsley and Cuttell, of the experience of the *Mission de France*, and of similar work being undertaken in Sheffield by Ted Wickham, the phrase "industrial mission" entered the language. To begin with, industrial mission took two forms, collaboration between clergy and the boards and managers of factories in evaluating working conditions and then negotiating improvements to ensure that employees were treated as sentient human beings, and also the systematic deployment of worker-priests. But, despite Cardinal Suhart's caveat, and despite the fact that the churches along the South London riverbank were virtually empty and that less than 5% of the population there had any sort of Church link, industrial mission attracted enemies as well as friends. It was accused of undermining the Church's parochial base, and this tension was long to remain an impediment to any general acceptance of its pastoral potential. In 1952 all the industrial work of the diocese was brought together as the South London Industrial Mission (SLIM), with Cuttell as its first "Padre" and George Giffin, the works manager at Siemens, as its first Chairman. Cuttell continued in post till 1962 when he was succeeded by Robert Gibson, and Gibson was succeeded in 1967 by Peter Challen.

Mervyn Stockwood was appointed Bishop of Southwark in 1959, and one of the three objectives which he set himself in his enthronement sermon was the creation of a "supplementary priesthood" which would enable clergy to be "alongside" people in their places of work. John Robinson, his newly appointed Bishop of Woolwich, was charged with developing this supplementary priesthood, and with starting up the Southwark Ordination Course (SOC), and SOC's central objective was to make it possible for men to train for the non-stipendiary ministry during their spare time without jeopardising their secular careers. Unlike the French worker-priests who were mostly educated men making a deliberate choice to work in menial jobs well beneath their capabilities, most of the ordinands on SOC intended to continue in their chosen careers. In order to make clear this fundamental distinction, they started calling themselves priest-workers rather than worker-priests. Priest-workers attached to clergy teams were an integral part of Stockwood's strategy for implementing another of his enthronement sermon objectives, the rejuvenation of the riverside parishes, but many of the early graduates of SOC chose to exercise a "ministry in secular employment" (MSE), seeing the focus of their ministry as being within the workplaces they had already chosen, and based in the parishes where they already lived. In 1968 a Chapter of Priest-Workers was established with David Wilson, a priest-baker, as its first Dean, and one of his successors was Barry Wright, a priest-Police Inspector, who later became the diocese's first MSE Canon (see page 62). In May 1980 Wright was present at the siege of the Iranian Embassy, and one of the SAS soldiers who was about to storm the building whispered to him, "Pray for us, Barry". On this occasion power of prayer proved efficacious, and there were no SAS casualties. From 1993 until his retirement in 2002 he was Services Chaplain to the Metropolitan Police. SOC graduates found themselves in the forefront of developing a theology of engagement in the world of secular work, and books which emerged from this process included "Working for the Kingdom" edited by Patrick Vaughan (1986) and "Rendering Unto Caesar" by Antony Hurst (also 1986). By 1990 the Diocesan Chapter of Priest-Workers had become so large that it was split into three, one for each episcopal area, with a Dean responsible for each. The MSE network nationally, which has always been ecumenical and has always owed a great deal to the Diocese of Southwark and to SOC, remained deliberately informal until July 1992, when a decision was made to establish CHRISM (Christians in Secular Ministry).

Stockwood also gave Robinson responsibility for the oversight of SLIM. During the 1960s, however, South London's industrial base was starting to decline, the victim both of its increasingly high overheads and of Government policies designed to bolster employment opportunities outside the capital. It took some time for conventional wisdom to appreciate what was happening, but Robinson and Challen became aware of it earlier than most. SLIM was expanded, and continued to work with employers to improve and humanise working conditions. It also extended its activities to include a great many enterprises, for example the Civil Service, whose activities could hardly be called "industrial", and at the same time widened its remit to include appraisal of the economy itself. As a part of this process Challen, with Robinson's active and sustained support, started to develop a "prophetic" ministry alongside the Mission's ongoing pastoral work aiming to research and publicise the side effects of employment, and to draw these to the attention of employers, the Trade Unions and the public generally. The consequences of systemic unemployment was one such side effect, and others included the collateral damage caused by working practices both to the local community and to the local environment. An important part of Challen's approach was the use of "social audit" which encouraged employers to publish accounts of the full spectrum of their profits and losses alongside their conventional financial balance sheets, and from this he developed the concept of "theological audit", working with individuals to enable them to assess their aspirations and actions in terms of their faith commitment.

Then, during the 1970s, the decline of South London's industry entered free fall, starting with the closure in 1970 of the Surrey Docks and its associated dockside industries. The effect, in sinister repetition of the years prior to the First World War, was the creation of an underclass of the socially excluded, people with no secure employment and who were denied, by virtue of their unemployment, the opportunity for finding any. SLIM continued to expand, and for most of the seventies and eighties its staffing complement was nine, seven of them ordained priests. It also became ecumenical, and included clergy from the Roman Catholic, Baptist, Methodist, Pentecostal and United Reformed Churches. Its lay members, known as "Associates", peaked at around two hundred, and were drawn from all denominations and from all forms of employment. During the 1970s industrial mission also had a strong presence in Croydon, then part of the Diocese of Canterbury, particularly under chaplains Michael Atkinson and David Cumber. Towards the end of Stockwood's episcopacy, however, not least because of Robinson's departure from the diocese, enthusiasm for industrial mission started to decline, and with it the resources voted to SLIM by Diocesan Synod, which remained inherently parish-focused. The advent of Area Mission Teams divided what remained of SLIM's shrinking chaplaincy resources, and similar pressures on the other denominations meant that their contribution and involvement also waned. Industrial mission returned to its roots with parochial clergy being encouraged to develop links with, and a ministry to, their "institutional parishioners".

During the 1980s under Margaret Thatcher, and during the 1990s under her successors, the nature of employment in South London again changed. There were no longer any large employers of manual workers along the riverside, but a new boom in other forms of economic activity more than compensated for this loss. There was an enormous increase in retailing, and unlovely superstores started mushrooming along the diocese's arterial roads, selling furniture, DIY materials, autoparts and even garden plants, often with associated restaurants in an attempt to make shopping a holistic experience. At the same time factories housing new forms of light industry were opened up in the southern part of the diocese, for example on the site of the long-disused Croydon airport. More significant, however, was the sea-change in the scope for making money in the City of London, especially in the aftermath of the "Big Bang" of October 1986 when the City was computerised and the demarcation of tasks between the distinct City professionals was brought to an end. London became one of the world's three time-zone financial centres along with Tokyo and New York, and of the three it was unquestionably the most truly international. The beneficiaries of the new wealth which this generated included a large number of commuters from the Diocese of Southwark's suburbia, and the City itself started to spill over onto the south bank of the river. This led to the creation of vast numbers of new jobs within the service sector, in restaurants, entertainment and fitness centres, and also in completely new fields of employment which earlier hadn't existed at all; the former warehouses and workshops of South London, and even the arches underneath its railway lines, started being converted into smart premises for small businesses engaged in graphic design, computer software development, conference organising, head-hunting, and later internet selling. All this continued South London's tradition for small scale innovation, but the skills required for entry into these new markets were sophisticated, and the stubborn pool of the socially excluded refused to disappear. Change has its shadow as well as its sunny side, and the need for change to be charted, evaluated, and responded to by the likes of industrial mission indubitably remains.

The Changing Role of Women

During the early years of the twentieth century most married women in the Diocese of Southwark were full-time wives and mothers, described in the census returns as "unoccupied" despite being grossly overworked within their households. Child bearing and child rearing were onerous tasks; women averaged six pregnancies resulting in between four and five live births, and children had to be managed without washing machines, disposable nappies, glass feeding-bottles, processed baby foods, prams or push chairs, and a great many other aids which today's mothers of babies take for granted. The maternal death rate associated with childbirth along the riverbank was still high, but a far bigger killer, particularly of younger women, was tuberculosis, a disease intimately linked with poor living conditions and poor diet. Access to medical attention was difficult for women who couldn't afford a doctor's fees. The Health Insurance Scheme introduced by Lloyd George in 1909 (see page 47) provided access to a panel doctor only for employed workers in recognised occupations who paid contributions and who were invariably men, and the only benefits for women were small maternity grants and free sanitorium care if they contracted TB. In poorer households where the husband was the only employed worker, the tradition was that he should receive more and better food than the women and children because of the household's dependence on his earnings, and female malnutrition was one of the major causes of TB. Even in households where the weekly wages were "tipped up" on the kitchen table, the man was generally allowed his beer money; more beer was drunk before the First World War than at any time later in the century, and the pub culture excluded women.

During the early years of the century very few of the married women in the commuter suburbs were in paid employment. Virtually all the women in employment were spinsters, most of them school teachers or nurses, two professions which were increasing both in numbers and in social prestige. Employment opportunities for working class women in South London were more plentiful than in many other parts of the country, particularly in shops, markets and factories, and in "domestic service" which, in the language of the census returns, included office cleaning. Armies of women were already crossing the river during the night to clean the offices in the City, many of them mothers who combined their night-work with being housewives during the day. Nearly all the larger houses in the semi-circle of commuter suburbs employed a young girl from a poorer part of the diocese as a live-in servant, working alongside the lady of the house.

When Women Went to Work, South Metropolitan Gas Works c 1916

In 1905 women were prohibited from voting in Parliamentary elections though, if they were householders, they were eligible to vote for their local authorities. The issue of female suffrage divided Edwardian society, and was argued about in all political parties and in all social classes, more often than not on the basis of prejudice rather than reason. The most effective campaigning was undertaken by the Union of Women's Suffrage Societies led by Millicent Garrett Fawcett, but better known because of its civil disobedience was the Women's Social and Political Union led by Emmeline Pankhurst and her daughters; the former were known as "suffragists" and the latter as "suffragettes". In 1912 Asquith's Liberal Government introduced a free-vote Bill which would have given all women the vote, but the Speaker ruled it unconstitutional and Asquith in consequence undertook to bring in women's suffrage when the Government next considered electoral reform. The First World War, however, intervened. Emmeline Pankhurst and her daughter Christabel made the transition from being disruptive activists to being compliant patriots, calling off their campaign almost with relief because they knew by then that their provocation of violence and their hunger strikes were becoming counter-effective, though her other daughter Sylvia became an angry pacifist and provoked the authorities into sending her back to prison. What actually precipitated women's suffrage was the contribution made by women to the war effort. Women had made good the labour shortage caused by male conscription, driving buses and trams and working in the munitions factories, and they had also joined the Armed Services, many of them serving overseas in the newly formed Women's Army Auxiliary Corps (WAACs), or as doctors in the Women's Hospital Corps, or as nurses in the Voluntary Aid Detachments (VADs). The pages of Punch, meanwhile, were being filled with jokes about the "servant problem" because live-in domestics were becoming much harder to find. The Reform Act of 1918 gave the vote to all women over thirty who were householders or the wives of householders. The age bar had nothing to do with women under thirty being thought less competent in casting their vote, but was introduced because the House of Commons was unwilling to contemplate an electorate in which women constituted a majority, and its ironic consequence was to deny suffrage to the very women who had contributed most to the war effort. Women were eventually put on an equal footing with men in 1928.

During the First World War women had been given a tantalising experience of paid employment, but they were sent back home as soon as the troops returned (see page 12). As unemployment gradually eased, so employment opportunities for women gradually expanded, particularly in secretarial and office work, though the work done by wives was invariably seen as secondary to the work done by their husbands. The Second World War again expanded the scope for women's employment, but this time the opportunities continued into peace time. The introduction of the Welfare State created whole new professions some of which were dominated by women, for example social work and occupational therapy, and it also expanded existing ones such as teaching and nursing. The assumption, though, was still that the mothers of small children would stay at home to look after them. The immigrant women who arrived in the 1950s found work in the Post Office and in London Transport, and were especially attracted to nursing which allowed them to train for a professional qualification whilst simultaneously getting paid.

And then came the 1960s. The liberation which followed the casting off of social convention coincided with the popular availability of the contraceptive pill, and women discovered that they no longer needed to perceive themselves as being subject to masculine control. The feminist movement encouraged them to discard their shackles and their bras, and the divorce rate soared; up till then most divorces had been initiated by men who had become attracted to another woman, but a majority of 1960s divorces were initiated by women who realised that alternatives existed to marriages which they perceived as no longer suiting them. Women also started to demand more interesting work and better working conditions, and campaigned for equal pay for equal work and for improved scope for job promotion. The Labour Government was sympathetic to their demands, and in 1975 passed the Sex Discrimination Act, and established the Equal Opportunities Commission to chivvy employers and to investigate complaints relating to gender discrimination. Most women who have recently become Old Age Pensioners remember the 1960s and 1970s as a period of tremulous excitement, of being able to rewrite the assumptions they had grown up with, and to expand their aspirations to include things they had thought would never become available to them. But they also tend to remember it as a period of great anxiety. They were having to stake out new territory without any adequate road map, and in particular they were having to juggle enhanced employment and leisure opportunities with their continuing responsibility for looking after their children; men were having to learn to cooperate with women as equals in the workplace, but very few husbands saw themselves as having a responsibility for child care equal to that of their wives. Nevertheless, this gender revolution has proved irreversible; employment opportunities for women have continued to expand, the glass ceiling which represents their level of maximum promotion is continually being raised, and no woman worth her salt is any longer willing to behave deferentially or to define herself as second class. John Major's "Back to Basics" campaign of 1992, a nostalgic and futile attempt to restore the pre-revolutionary values of the 1950s, cut very little ice and affected the attitudes of very few women. But the anxieties continue too; the juggling act required by the conflicting responsibilities of employment and child care gets no easier and causes many women to postpone motherhood and some to forego it altogether, and uncertainty about the rules that govern sexual relationships generates much more insecurity amongst women than amongst men.

Two professional groups which were specifically excluded from the provisions of the Sex Discrimination Act were midwives and the clergy, and men were admitted to midwifery earlier than women were admitted to the Church of England priesthood. Despite their valuable but largely unacknowledged contributions, women in the Church of England were allowed to perform no formal role within its structures between its foundation in Tudor times and the middle of Queen Victoria's reign. During the 1840s a number of Christian women's groups were founded which played an active part in the development of social welfare programmes but, when the moment came for these activities to be incorporated within the Church's structures, the positions of responsibility were always given to men; Florence Nightingale is an example of a woman who decided to pursue her Christian vocation independently of the Church. The 1860s saw the start of a number of Anglican sisterhoods, and in 1862 the Order of Deaconesses was refounded within the Church of England, and refounded in what was to become the Diocese of Southwark (see page 77). Training centres for deaconesses were established, first in Clapham and later at Greyladies in Blackheath and, up till the Second World War, deaconesses in their cassocks and veils were a common sight throughout the diocese, and they were greatly respected. One of the most respected, and most remarkable, was Cecilia Goodenough, who was appointed Warden of Talbot Settlement in Camberwell in 1936, and whose continuing ministry included heading up Greyladies whilst working for SLIM, and becoming a founder-lecturer on SOC.

During the demoralising days of the war the deaconesses of the diocese did much to hold things together, making good the shortage of clergy manpower and making, doing and mending in the temporary buildings which were having to be used where the churches had been bombed. After the war, however, things began to change. Many deaconesses decided to take secular jobs and to shed their uniforms, and there were the beginnings of rumblings of dissatisfaction that ordination as a deaconess was a second class ordination. Nevertheless, one remarkable aspect of the episcopacy of Mervyn Stockwood was the extent to which the admission of women to the priesthood was never an issue. One might have expected that Stockwood's progressive ideas and the emergence of the feminist movements would have put women's ordination at least onto the agenda, but most of the practical women of the diocese like Anne Gurney and Gwen Rymer seem to have been content with continuing with getting on with their jobs. The campaign for women's ordination got under way in earnest in the early 1970s with the setting up of the Christian Parity Group; it included three Southwark women in prominent positions, Una Kroll, Monica Furlong and Elsie Baker. The issue was debated in General Synod in 1978, but the proposition failed to gain the necessary two-thirds majorities in all three Houses, and at the end of the debate Una Kroll famously shouted from the gallery: "We asked for bread but you gave us a stone. Long live God". Some ground was gained, however, with Synod resolving that there was no specifically theological objection to women becoming priests. In 1979 the Movement for the Ordination of Women was established to coordinate a more systematic campaign, and a strategy was developed. In July 1980 an ordination service at St Paul's Cathedral was disrupted by Monica Furlong and others, but Archbishop Runcie wrote to her afterwards saying that, whilst he could not condone the disruption, he was sympathetic to her cause. The Women Deacons Measure, passed in 1985 and implemented two years later, allowed women to be ordained deacon on the same basis as men, and a celebration of women's ministries was held in Canterbury Cathedral in 1986 at which those present tantalisingly included ordained women from other denominations and from Anglican provinces overseas.

Then, on 11 November 1992, triggered by a motion initially tabled by the Diocese of Southwark, came the great debate in General Synod. The elections to Synod membership had been fought almost exclusively on the issue of women's ordination, and virtually all the candidates both for the House of Clergy and for the House of Laity had declared their positions to their electorates. It was clear that the voting was going to be very close, and both sides mounted strong campaigns in an effort both to sway the floating voters and to influence public opinion beyond the Church's confines. Significant speeches were made in the debate by June Osborne, who presented the case for MOW, and by Roy Williamson, Bishop of Southwark, who stated that he saw women's ordination as a matter of justice, and justice as an issue for the Kingdom. "Just as the New Testament bids us have as high a doctrine of ministry as we like so long as our doctrine of the Church is higher", he said, quoting John Robinson, "so it also commands us to have as high a doctrine of the Church as we may provided that our doctrine of the Kingdom is higher". But perhaps the most influential speech came from Mark Santer, Bishop of Birmingham, who said that he had initially opposed the measure on the grounds that it would do perhaps irreparable harm to the Church of England's relationship with Rome, but then had had to change his mind because he had come to see his pastoral obligations towards the women of his diocese as deserving a higher priority. In the event the voting was indeed very close, but the necessary two-thirds majorities were achieved in all three Houses, and the following morning an immortal banner headline in The Sun proclaimed to the nation, "CHURCH SAYS YES TO VICARS IN KNICKERS".

There was still more work that needed to be done, however, both to pacify those who discovered themselves to be on the losing side, and also to prepare women for their admission to the priesthood and to prepare Church members for women's priestly ministry. The Bishops issued their Manchester Statement in 1993 which provided for Provincial Episcopal Visitors, or "flying bishops", to exercise an episcopal oversight of clergy who wanted to remain uncontaminated by hands that had ordained a woman, and the Roman Catholic Church made special arrangements for the admission to its priesthood of Anglican clergy who had chosen to convert, including some who were married. Clergy who chose to resign their orders were financially compensated, and the group of "antis" called "Cost of Conscience" renamed themselves "Forward in Faith". And then, in the Spring of 1994, the great moment of women's ordination to the priesthood arrived. Bishop Williamson had a busy time; not only was he called upon to ordain almost a hundred women, in three separate batches, in Southwark Cathedral, but he was also summoned over the river to ordain the first women priests at St Paul's because of the reluctance to officiate of some of the London bishops, including David Hope then the Diocesan and Richard Chartres then Bishop of Stepney. The oldest woman ordained priest in Southwark, indeed the oldest woman in the country to be ordained to the priesthood at that time was Elsie Baker, then aged eighty-four. She had applied for deaconess training at Greyladies in 1929 but had been made to wait, and had eventually been made deaconess just before the war. She had spent the war years first looking after the parish of All Saints Tooting, and then doing her best to hold together the parish of All Saints Walworth where the church had been destroyed by bombing. Told after the war that the Church no longer required her services, she moved on to teach RE at a secondary school in Sydenham and soon became head of the department. Shortly after John Robinson had arrived as Bishop of Woolwich she was made Warden of Greyladies, by then known as Dartmouth House, and a member of the Blackheath Team Ministry. Williamson went to see her shortly before her ordination and said to her, "Elsie, I'm sorry but I can't make you a priest". "I suppose", she replied sadly, "that at my age I couldn't really have expected it". "No", said Bishop Roy, "I can ordain you, but God made you a priest a very long time ago". She died in 2003.

The first women priests inevitably encountered difficulties, but probably fewer in the Diocese of Southwark than in other parts of the country. Congregations needed to make adjustments because even MOW supporters found the experience of receiving Communion from the hands of a woman unusual, and the women themselves needed to make adjustments too as they accommodated to their newly acquired role. But on the whole it all worked quite remarkably well, and nowadays it is hard to believe that all that drama was happening only ten years ago. Southwark Cathedral appointed Helen Cunliffe as the country's first woman canon in 1995, Christine Hardman is now Archdeacon of Lewisham, and women incumbents are commonplace throughout the diocese. Women as bishops? They already exist within the Anglican Communion in New Zealand, Canada and the United States, and it is difficult to imagine that their arrival will long be delayed within the Church of England, or that the enabling procedures will have so turbulent a passage.

Health and Social Security

The population of South London in 1905 was divided roughly equally between the lower middle classes of the railway suburbs and the poor along the riverbank. The lower middle classes weren't rich, but they earned enough to keep up the mortgage payments on their newly built terraced houses and to buy food for their families. Along the riverbank, however, the average working man's pay was "round about a pound a week" which made feeding the family and paying the rent a perpetual struggle, and a nightmare whenever the pound a week was not forthcoming. Insanitary housing and inadequate diet meant that killer diseases like tuberculosis, diphtheria, scarlet fever, influenza and pneumonia were rife, and that miscarriages, still-births and infant mortality were all commonplace. A frequent question in both parts of the diocese was "can we afford the doctor?", and along the riverbank the answer was all too often "no". The alternative was to buy patent remedies at the neighbourhood chemist, but most of these were based on quinine and so caused almost as many problems as they solved.

The true nature of poverty was beginning to be systematically investigated and understood, and was therefore becoming less susceptible to the prejudices of the people who looked down on it from further up the social spectrum. The most influential study was Joseph Rowntree's "Poverty - A Study of Town Life", published in 1901 and based on house-to-house surveys in York, which looked first at household income, and then the quantity and type of food necessary for sustaining health, and then at the extent to which families could afford to buy it. Rowntree distinguished between what he called "primary poverty" where household income was simply insufficient, and what he called "secondary poverty" where inadequate diet was a consequence of unwise spending. His study and others like it underpinned what came to be called the "Social Programme", and the Social Programme was adopted by the Liberal Party and played its part in winning them their massive General Election victory in 1905. It was this Liberal Government which brought in the biggest statutory changes to people's welfare of the twentieth century, bigger even than the introduction of the Welfare State, although implementation of them had to await two further General Elections and the death of a king. The Liberals' Chancellor of the Exchequer was David Lloyd George, and his "People's Budget" of 1909 was the first systematic attempt to redistribute income by taxing the rich and spending it on the poor. The Budget's passage through Parliament, however, was blocked by the Tory majority in the House of Lords. Herbert Asquith, who had succeeded Campbell-Bannerman as Prime Minister in 1908, called a General Election in January 1910 which he won with a slightly reduced majority, but the House of Lords again rejected the Budget. Asquith asked King Edward VII to create peers in order to ensure the Budget's passage, but the King refused. Edward VII then died in May, and the new King George V agreed that in such circumstances the creation of peers was constitutionally reasonable. A second General Election in December of the same year gave Asquith his necessary mandate, and in 1911 the Parliament Act was passed which significantly limited the House of Lords' powers, and in particular their powers over Budgets. The passage of the Act was supported by the bench of Bishops led by Archbishop Randall Davidson, dispelling early in the century the myth that the Church of England was the Tory Party at prayer. Interestingly, the peers whom the King would have created included such luminaries as Bertrand Russell, Sir Robert Baden-Powell, Thomas Hardy and J.M.Barrie, all of whom would indubitably have improved the Upper House's calibre.

The Parliament Act made possible the passing of the National Insurance Act of 1911 which implemented the People's Budget's intentions. The Act and its momentous consequences were a collaborative effort between two future Prime Ministers whom one would not instinctively think of as a team, Lloyd George and Winston Churchill, who was then the Liberals' President of the Board of Trade. Lloyd George established Health Insurance, which he admitted was actually sickness insurance and he jokingly referred to the way in which insurance against death was called life insurance, and Churchill established Unemployment Benefit. Up till then, responsibility for providing assistance in cases of need had remained vested in the local Boards of Guardians under the provisions of Elizabethan Poor Law, and it was these archaic arrangements which Churchill replaced. His system of Unemployment Benefit was based on a compulsory liability for joint insurance contributions by employers and employees, and then entitlement to benefit conditional only upon registering at a Labour Exchange; he had established Labour Exchanges in 1908 with the help of a young adviser named William Beveridge. To begin with, access to benefits in instances of sickness or unemployment was confined to certain registered occupations but, as time went by, more and more occupations were brought within the scope of the schemes, and entitlement to benefit was progressively expanded. The extent of the prejudice against these measures was exemplified by the virulent opposition to them of John Burns, the flamboyant and radical New Liberal MP for Battersea who had earlier led the unsuccessful dockers' strike of 1889; Burns had difficulty in stomaching the prospect of the "undeserving poor" being brought up to the level of the deserving. Unemployment Benefit later came under enormous pressure during the early 1920s when the numbers of people out of work soared, and in 1924 Ramsey MacDonald's Labour Government introduced National Assistance to supplement it through making additional payments in cases of proven need. In 1935 Baldwin's Conservative Government set up the Unemployment Assistance Board which paid out benefits to the unemployed solely on a means-tested basis. The means-testing was made deliberately harsh and was deeply resented, and one of the most appalling stories about it tells of a family of four in Peckham who owned six chairs but were told that they had to sell two of them before any benefit would be paid.

The main effect of Lloyd George's Health Insurance scheme was that it established Sickness Benefit, and it had remarkably little to do with health; its only health care provision was that it allowed free access for registered workers to a salaried "panel doctor". Initially the registered workers were invariably men, though it was women who really needed access to health care (see page 41) and they could only receive free help if they contracted tuberculosis. There were, however, a small number of doctors with social consciences who practised in the poorer areas of the Diocese of Southwark, and who were prepared to make do on very little income. One of the most remarkable was Albert Salter who, while a young medical student at Guy's, had been shocked by the living conditions he encountered around him. He and his wife decided to live in Bermondsey rather than in any of the more affluent suburbs which they could easily have afforded, and he soon felt compelled to enter politics. He was elected to the Bermondsey Borough Council as a New Liberal but later switched to Labour, and as Mayor of Bermondsey led the Council in its many radical initiatives which seriously embarrassed Governments of both right and left (see page 8). In 1924 he was elected Bermondsey's first Labour MP, and was succeeded as Mayor by his wife who thus became London's first woman Mayor; the first act of her mayoralty, in her capacity as Bermondsey's returning officer, was to announce her husband's election to the Commons. The Salters suffered a personal tragedy which neither of them ever forgot. They had decided not only to live in Bermondsey but also to send their only daughter Joyce to the local Board School, but while a pupil there she caught tuberculosis and died at the age of seven. There is a very moving statue by Diane Gorvin on the Thames Path at Bermondsey Wall entitled "Dr Salter's Dream" which shows him as a very old man sitting on a bench and looking across the path towards an image of his daughter, still a little girl of seven in a long Edwardian dress with a bow at the back.

One of the anomalies of the pre-NHS South London riverbank was that it was very poorly endowed with community medical services but very well endowed with teaching hospitals. St Thomas's Hospital had started its long life as the hospice of St Mary Overie (see page 70), and Guy's had been established in 1725 on the opposite side of St Thomas's Street when the capacity of the older hospital had become inadequate for local needs (see page 74). For the next hundred years the two hospitals ran a combined medical school, and the apothecary's certificate awarded to the poet John Keats, whose temporary residence in St Thomas's Street is recorded by a blue plaque, shows him as having graduated from "The Hospital of St Thomas's and Guy's". Florence Nightingale, in the aftermath of her triumphant return from the Crimean War, learned that St Thomas's was about to be redeveloped, and therefore chose it as the hospital in which to found her School of Nursing. She then helped to design the new state-of-the-art building just downstream from Lambeth Palace into which St Thomas's moved in 1862. The vacated site in St Thomas's Street was acquired in 1869 by Baron Ferdinand de Rothschild, a rich philanthropist in the Thomas Guy tradition, and on it he built the nation's first hospital specially for children, naming it in memory of his wife Evelina. The Evelina Children's Hospital continued in business till 1976 when it became a ward within the newly built Guy's Hospital tower, and it is now in the process of relocating to St Thomas's. The old St Thomas's site used to include St Thomas's Church, now deconsecrated, and the church building's refurbishment in 1975 was the occasion of one of the most extraordinary finds in the field of medical archaeology; between its roof and the church's ceiling was discovered an abandoned operating theatre dating from 1822, complete with buckets of sawdust to mop up the blood. It is now open to the public as a medical museum.

The pattern during the nineteenth century and the first half of the twentieth was for teaching hospitals to be located in areas where there were plenty of poor patients on

Nurses from Guy's Hospital in Southwark Cathedral celebrating the hospital's bicentenary in 1925

whom the students could practise, and then for most of the students to move away as soon as they had qualified. The Medical School of King's College had been started in Lincoln's Inn Fields in 1829, and it crossed the river to Denmark Hill in 1913. The large houses around Camberwell Green, which had formerly been affluent, were at that time multi-occupied slums inhabited by suitably impoverished potential patients, though the area has more recently been restored to something resembling its earlier glory. Just opposite King's is another of South London's teaching hospitals, the Bethlem and Maudsley. The Bethlem has its origins in the notorious lunatic asylum which was initially housed in the building that is now the Imperial War Museum in Kennington, and which was a tourist attraction during the eighteenth century when watching the lunatics was considered a fashionable spectator sport. In 1980 South London gained yet another teaching hospital when the medical school at St George's vacated its prestigious premises at Hyde Park Corner and also crossed the river, in its case to Tooting.

During the 1920s and 1930s the health of the nation gradually improved, particularly in South London's outer ring of newly built suburbs, without any dramatic changes being made to the arrangements through which health care was delivered. Then came one of the most extraordinary phenomena of the twentieth century, the spirit of reform which pervaded the country during the Second World War, a determined commitment to sweeping away all the old disparities of class and income, and to remodelling society along lines that were fair, efficient and rational. This spirit manifested itself in Sir Patrick Abercrombie's Greater London Plan (see page 16) and in the Butler Education Act of 1944 (see page 55), but its most significant manifestations were in the fields of social security and health. The programme's moving spirit was an older and now knighted Sir William Beveridge, and he had the intellect and perspicacity to pull together all the various strands of existing service provision and to recast them into a seamless and logical whole, stretching, as he put it, "from the cradle to the grave". Old Age Pensions were introduced for men aged over sixty-five and for women aged over sixty, and Family Allowances for all the children in every family after the eldest, breaking new ground by being made payable not to the father but to the mother.

The 1945 Labour Government's first Minister for Health and Housing was Aneurin Bevan, the son of a Welsh coal miner and a former coal miner himself, and to him fell the task of introducing and then implementing the 1948 National Health Service Act. He brought together the patchwork of hospitals which predated the Act within a unified and coordinated management structure, and made everybody who worked in them NHS employees. His most difficult problem was winning the support of the medical profession, but he managed it by a combination of his notorious Welsh charm and a series of concessions which allowed hospital doctors to treat private patients in NHS hospitals, and which remunerated General Practitioners through a capitation allowance rather than a contract of employment. Beveridge's naive hope was that, once an initial backlog of health underprovision had been rectified, NHS expenditure could be maintained at a steady state. It quickly became evident, however, that the scale of underprovision was far greater than he had realised, and that the consequence of access to health services that were "free at point of delivery" was an enormous increase both in expectation and in demand; during each of the two years that followed the implementation of the 1948 Act expenditure on the health service was 40% greater than had been budgeted for. Because of this, and because of the unexpected demands being made on the Government at the time to finance world-wide peace-keeping operations, the Chancellor of the Exchequer Sir Stafford Cripps found it necessary in 1951 to introduce charges for spectacles and for false teeth, and Bevan, even though no longer the Minister for Health, found it necessary to resign in protest at what he saw as a betrayal of principle. His resignation was one of the factors which brought Churchill back to Downing Street in the 1951 General Election, but the Conservatives committed themselves to retaining the NHS, and throughout the thirteen years of Tory rule that followed they continued to expand and improve it; two of the most dedicated Ministers for Health were Iain Macleod and Enoch Powell, and Powell's interventions included an attempt to alleviate the chronic shortage of nurses by recruiting in the West Indies (see page 31).

Even more remarkable than the longevity of Sir William Beveridge was the longevity of Joseph Rowntree. He had published "Poverty - A Study of Town Life" in 1901, and in 1951 he published a sequel entitled "Poverty and the Welfare State" in which his upbeat assessment, half a century on, was that poverty had at long last been eliminated. Ten years later, however, poverty was rediscovered. Help the Aged was set up in 1961 to press for better provision for the elderly, and it was followed by other campaigning groups, most notably the Child Poverty Action Group in 1965. The lead in the scientific charting of the nation's poverty passed from Rowntree to the London School of Economics, and in particular to Professors Richard Titmuss and Brian Abel-Smith who published, in 1965, an influential study called "The Poor and the Poorest". Rowntree had used an absolute measure in defining poverty, concerning himself with whether family income was sufficient to allow the purchase of life's necessities, but the criteria used by the LSE were relative; what mattered to Titmuss and Abel-Smith was the extent of the gap between the rich and the poor. The 1964 Labour Government, which had been powerfully influenced by the LSE research, was fully aware that the existing levels of National Assistance and the Old Age Pension left many people relatively badly off, and its response in 1966 was the introduction of arrangements for making discretionary top-up payments called Supplementary Benefit. Even though "Sup Ben" had a very long run for its money, the difficulties inherent in the system very soon became apparent. Claimants who were refused benefit started asking why they had been turned down, and it became necessary to make public the criteria against which eligibility for discretionary payments was decided and, once the criteria had been published, clients became able to make their claims in ways which made their eligibility more likely. The result was that expenditure soared; Claimants' Unions began to be organised, and a whole new profession came into being based around helping claimants to maximise their benefit entitlement. A particularly difficult issue was housing costs; whereas the cost of food and clothing was pretty well constant throughout the country, housing costs varied greatly from one area to another. Housing costs were therefore taken out of the benefit system, and new arrangements called Housing Benefit were introduced; Housing Benefit was administered by local authorities who were assumed to have better local knowledge than the DHSS, and the local authorities were then reimbursed by the Government for most of what they had paid out. Many local authorities, however, found these procedures very difficult to implement, and the Borough of Lambeth in particular got into such a mess with its Housing Benefit account that the Government had to be called in to run it. Gradually the old system of discretionary payments was effectively abandoned, and a raft of new means-tested benefits like the Social Fund and Family Credit were introduced together with a complementary raft of tax credits, all of them complex but at least clear and cash-limited. The new bugbears became the "perverse incentive" and the "poverty trap", and many people came to realise that there were circumstances in which they would be better off if they earned less or nothing at all.

Another of Beveridge's naive assumptions was that the NHS would be inherently fair and efficient, but it soon became clear that it was going to be neither. One problem was that too many decisions on the allocation of resources were made by inherently conservative and self-interested doctors, and in 1974 David Owen, Minister for Health in the newly elected Labour Government and himself a qualified doctor, embarked upon two projects to make the allocation of resources fairer and better geared to meeting the nation's health care needs. One was called QALYs, and the other was called RAWP. QALY stood for Quality Adjusted Life Year, and the research on which QALYs were based enabled decisions to be made as to which health procedures resulted in the greatest benefit to patients and the best value for money. And RAWP stood for the Resource Allocation Working Party, which made recommendations as to how expenditure per patient could be made fairer. RAWP required South London to forfeit a great deal of money because its big teaching hospitals were so inordinately expensive but, because the South London Health Authorities initially found it easier to make savings on community health services, it became necessary for them to develop a Regional RAWP to divert resources back into the community. A consequence of this readjustment was the closure of a large number of South London's smaller hospitals, including some of the long-stay psychiatric hospitals which had been built at the end of the nineteenth century at what had then been London's outer edges; the euphemism for this process was "care in the community", and a great many psychiatric patients who had become institutionalised were discharged without much in the way of alternative provision for them having been put in place.

The other problem was the NHS's inherent inefficiency. The Thatcher Government which came to power in 1979 assumed this to be a consequence of there being too little scope for consumer choice or for the free play of market forces, but even Margaret Thatcher was unwilling to abandon the basic principle of access to the NHS being free at point of delivery. The essence of her reforms was that patients should be given greater freedom in choosing their GP, GPs greater freedom in choosing the hospitals to which their patients were referred, and hospitals greater freedom in responding to the demands

Archiepiscopal Tudor, Lambeth Palace SE1

Late Eighteenth Century Desirable Classical, Kennington SE 11

Late Nineteenth Century Railway Commuter Terracing, Nunhead SE15

Early Twentieth Century Municipalism, Deptford SE8

1920's William Morris Rustic, Well Hall SE9

1930's Art Deco Semi-detached, Kingston Bypass

1970's GLC Brutalism, Heygate Estate SE17

1990's Resurrected Warehousing, Shad Thames SE1

made on them. The Labour Government elected in 1997 continued to adhere to these principles, and present developments to do with Fund-holding GPs and Foundation Hospitals are attempts to put them into practice. Another aspect of Margaret Thatcher's efforts to make the NHS more efficient was privatisation, based on the assumption that the private sector was better at management than the public sector, and many ancillary hospital services started being "contracted out".

Visiting the sick has always been a part of the job description of Church of England clergy, and prior to the 1948 National Health Service Act some hospitals employed their own chaplains. The 1948 Act formalised this responsibility by establishing a Hospital Chaplaincy Service, with its chaplains employed by the Hospital Management Boards. This placed Church of England chaplains in a position of divided accountability, to their Hospital Board and to their Bishop, but it caused very few difficulties in practice at least in part because of an overriding assumption that the primary loyalty of clergy was to the parochial ministry; clergy were required to do at least five years in a parish before taking up a hospital appointment, and after five years as a hospital chaplain they would go back to a parish. The main focus of the chaplains' ministry was to patients and their families, and this again was not too different from their parochial experience. This pattern started to change in the mid 1960s during Mervyn Stockwood's episcopacy, and it started to change initially in the large psychiatric hospitals where the harbingers were Derek Blows at Warlingham Park and Leslie Virgo at Cane Hill. The long-stay psychiatric hospitals were close to being total institutions, and the staff were almost as institutionalised as the patients. Blows and Virgo saw their ministry as being to the whole hospital community, which meant working with the staff as well as with the patients, and which also meant taking an interest in the management structure of the hospital and in the ways in which its services were organised and delivered. This pattern of chaplaincy soon spread to the large teaching hospitals, and by the mid 1970s it had become the standard pattern of Health Care Chaplaincy; the name had had to be changed in order to fit the chaplains' new job description. Another change that happened during the mid 1970s was that the DHSS revised its arrangements for determining chaplaincy establishment. Instead of establishment being derived from the numbers of patients of declared denominations, Health Authorities were given delegated responsibility for making their own decisions as to how many chaplains to employ and on what basis. This meant that the chaplaincy had to compete for resources against the whole gamut of other demands on health care expenditure. Prophets of doom were confounded, however, and most Health Authorities, and also their successor NHS Trusts, decided that the employment of chaplains represented a sensible investment and good value for money. This change hastened the trend towards a more holistic ministry within the Health Service, and chaplains found themselves playing a more central role in service planning and delivery, for example in developing human resources policies and in devising protocols both for research and for clinical ethics. Three chaplains who played a pivotal role in bringing about these changes were Neville Smith at Guy's, Ian Ainsworth-Smith at St George's, and John Foskett at the Bethlem and Maudsley, and at the same time they helped to establish health care chaplaincy as a career structure in its own right instead of it being seen merely as a temporary digression from the parochial ministry.

Unsurprisingly, this development in health care chaplaincy had consequences for theology. Hospitals have always been places where human beings are forced to confront life's most traumatic issues, and increasing numbers of people do not have the background of a faith community's traditions of liturgy or ritual which can help them to come to terms with what is happening; everybody has spiritual needs, but not everybody has access to religious tradition. As employees of secular institutions, health care chaplains are now required to minister to people of all faiths and none, and are not permitted to confine their work to people of their own denomination. During the 1980s and 1990s chaplains found themselves working first ecumenically and then with people of other faiths, and in particular helping the Muslim community to develop its own chaplaincy equivalent. And chaplains also started becoming involved in helping people with no access to religious language or religious ritual to find ways of coming to terms with death, whether the prospect of their own or that of a close relative or friend. And this lacuna in language and ritual also became apparent when people had to face, for example, a still-birth or a pregnancy termination. The lessons that chaplains learned from this aspect of their work were then valuably fed back to NHS management, to NHS front-line staff, and also to parochial clergy. Today there are about forty health care chaplains, full and part-time, employed within the Diocese of Southwark, more than in any other diocese apart from London. Most are employed in hospitals but some work solely in the community, for example as Mental Health Chaplains in the aftermath of the closure of the large psychiatric hospitals. Largely as a consequence of preparatory work done by Foskett, the Bethlem and Maudsley now has a John Robinson Research Fellow who is exploring the links between depth psychology and religious belief.

And there is one other area of health care in which institutions within the Diocese of Southwark have played an important national role. During the 1870s, following the revival of Anglican sisterhoods, the Hostel of God was founded on Clapham Common to care specifically for people who were dying. Then, almost a century later, a remarkable woman started a similar hospice in Sydenham called St Christopher's, because it was St Christopher who carried the Christ-child from one side of life's river to the other. In 1973 Dame Cicely Saunders brought together the only three terminal care hospices which existed in England at the time, her own, the Hostel of God which had changed its name to Trinity Hospice, and St Joseph's, a Roman Catholic hospice in Hackney, and in partnership they organised a national conference to promote the creation of a hospice network. The initiative worked, and all the other terminal care hospices in the country, including St Raphael in Cheam, owe their origin to Dame Cicely's foresight and to that 1973 conference. Much of the ethos of the hospice movement is a consequence of research undertaken at St Christopher's by Dr Colin Murray Parkes, in particular on the support of bereaved relatives and on the alleviation of pain through morphine-based drugs, and it also underpins much of the palliative work undertaken both in hospitals and in the community.

Education

Sherlock Holmes, riding in a train from Clapham Junction to Victoria in one of Sir Arthur Conan Doyle's stories, invites Dr Watson to admire "those big, isolated buildings rising above the slates like brick islands in a lead coloured sea". "The Board Schools?", asks Watson, with his usual naivety. "Lighthouses, my boy!", remonstrates Holmes, "beacons of the future, capsules with hundreds of bright little seeds in each, out of which will spring the wiser, better England of the future". The same railway journey can still be made today. The view has changed little, and the roofs of what used to be the Board Schools are still clearly visible breaking the skyline. And Holmes's point still stands.

The Board Schools which were the focus of Sherlock Holmes's hopes for the future were the creation of the Forster Education Act of 1870, which brought in compulsory elementary education for all children between the ages of five and fourteen. Prior to 1870, however, more than half the nation's children were already receiving some sort of education, and significantly more than half in the area that was later to become the Diocese of Southwark. A number of schools in South London had been founded in Elizabethan and Jacobean times, some of them with monastic origins dating from the Middle Ages. Kingston Grammar School, which claims to be the oldest, started in its Lovekyn Chantry in the thirteenth century, and in 1561 was refounded after the Chantry's dissolution. St Saviour's Grammar School and St Olave's Grammar School were founded in 1571 and 1562 respectively, though they later amalgamated, and Whitgift in Croydon started in 1596. In 1619 the actor-manager Edward Alleyn founded his College of God's Gift for twelve poor scholars in Dulwich, and these poor scholars became the academic ancestors of today's pupils at Dulwich College, Alleyn's, and James Allen's Girls School. Three schools have links with St Martin-in-the-Fields in Trafalgar Square, two as a consequence of the dwindling of the child population of the West End. St Martin-in-the-Fields in Tulse Hill began as that church's Elizabethan Grammar School, and Archbishop Tenison's in Kennington started its life in Leicester Square where it had been founded by Thomas Tenison when vicar of St Martin's in the seventeenth century. The diocese's other Archbishop Tenison's, in Croydon, was founded by Tenison when he was living in Addiscombe after his appointment by William III as Archbishop of Canterbury. Most of the children in formal education in 1870, however, attended schools which had been established as charitable institutions by Church of England or Roman Catholic parishes around the middle of the nineteenth century. A large majority of these Church schools provided only rudimentary education in the three Rs with a view to enabling their children to obtain employment as artisans, shopkeepers or domestic servants, but a few had Grammar School status and educated children up to the age of eighteen, preparing some of them for university entrance; University College London had been founded in 1826 and King's College three years later, and in 1878 UCL became the first university in the country to admit women students, significantly earlier than Oxford or Cambridge.

In the same way that the 1948 National Health Service Act encountered difficulties in grafting a universal national health service onto a haphazard amalgam of existing local provision, so Forster also encountered difficulties in grafting his new national education system onto the amalgam of existing schools. The Liberal Party of which he was a member included a strong Nonconformist element, and there was much wrangling within Cabinet about how best to bring the denominational schools into the new system without discriminating unduly in the Church of England's favour. The compromise, which Prime Minister Gladstone thoroughly disapproved of though felt bound to accept, was that the School Boards were allowed to pay for poor children to be educated in denominational schools, but that specifically denominational teaching was not permitted in the schools managed directly by the Boards except by Ministers of Religion who had been invited in and who were not remunerated by the Boards. For the remainder of the nineteenth century the denominational issue remained buried only just below the surface, and it came to a head once more in 1902 when the Balfour Education Act, a Conservative measure, transferred responsibility for education from the *ad hoc* School Boards to the local authorities, and introduced the system for funding education directly from the rates. Anti-Catholic prejudice immediately showed itself in anger at the

The Board School Effect, Paragon School, Searles Road SE1 c 1905

prospect of "Rome on the Rates", but there was also considerable opposition from within the Liberal Party over what was seen as a requirement on Free Church rate-payers to subsidise the Church of England. When the Liberals regained power in 1906 they committed themselves to addressing this anomaly, but the McKenna Bill of 1908, which attempted to steer a middle course between the Nonconformist diehards on the Liberal backbenches in the Commons and the Anglican Bishops in the House of Lords, pleased no one; the Bill failed, significantly weakening the Campbell-Bannerman Government in the process, and the Balfour Act remained in force, barely amended, for more than forty years.

The Butler Education Act was passed in 1944, and when Rab Butler eventually retired from politics in 1964 he looked back on it as his greatest achievement. The Act was an important part of the vision of the "New Jerusalem" which inspired the nation during the latter part of the Second World War, envisaging the withering away of the old divisions of class and wealth, and the opening up of equality of opportunity for all. Butler thought that he had succeeded in banishing the spectre of denominationalism which had haunted educational debate in Britain for so long; the proportion of children being educated in Church of England schools dropped to one in three, but the proportion in Roman Catholic schools actually increased, and the issue raised its head two decades later when Roman Catholic schools were perceived as favouring the descendants of Irish immigrants at the expense of the descendants of immigrants from the New Commonwealth. Butler also proposed raising the school leaving age to fifteen, but the implementation of this had to be delayed until 1947. Most importantly, however, he introduced a change of school at eleven from Primary to Secondary with three options for secondary education, Grammar Schools, Technical Schools and Modern Schools. The initial thinking was that 5% of children should go to Grammar Schools, roughly the proportion at the time, 15% to Technical Schools, and 80% to Modern Schools, but the aspiration of a great many parents during the New Jerusalem era was that their children should receive a better education than they had, and this put pressure on the local authorities to provide Grammar School places for a great many more than 5%. By the mid-1950s the proportion of children going to Grammar Schools had settled at 25%, with Technical Schools, which got off the ground only in a small number of local authority areas none of them in South London, taking less than 5%, and Secondary Moderns the remaining 70%. In one sense this was a great improvement, since the chances of a working class child getting into university, which had been one in a hundred prior to World War I, improved to one in ten. But in another sense, which had not been anticipated, it actually institutionalised and reinforced class differences because it meant that, by and large, it was the 25% of children who came from middle-class backgrounds who got the 25% Grammar School places.

The issue of selection for Grammar School places dominated educational debate throughout the fifties and sixties. Selection was made on the basis of academic aptitude, and an aptitude test had been developed known as the Eleven Plus. Butler and his early apologists insisted that there was no question of the Eleven Plus being "passed" or "failed", since its intention was to ensure that round pegs got fitted into round holes, but this was not how it was perceived by middle-class parents. Middle-class parents were desperate to ensure that their children passed the Eleven Plus since a Grammar School education would ensure the retention of their middle-class status, and this anxiety manifested itself in cramming for the aptitude tests, and in demands for retakes whenever the test was failed. And the proportion of Grammar School places inexorably rose. Within the Labour Party the Eleven Plus was seen as socially divisive and therefore as politically unacceptable, and Labour's manifesto for its election victory in 1964 included a commitment to its abolition, and with it the abolition of Grammar Schools. The 1944 Act did in fact include provision for local authorities to provide Comprehensive Schools, and over two hundred had been established prior to Labour's victory, all by Labour authorities including several by the LCC; two of the earliest in South London were Kidbrooke in Eltham and Mayfield in Putney, both carefully situated at points where "slum and suburb met" in order to ensure an acceptable social mix.

Anthony Crosland, Labour's incoming Minister for Education, was immediately confronted with the issue of how to set about requiring local authorities to "go Comprehensive", and the device he hit upon was the issue of Circular 10/65 which required authorities, not to introduce Comprehensive Schools, but to draw up plans for the introduction of Comprehensive Schools. Throughout most of the country this did the trick and, except in a few die-hard Conservative authorities which included Kent where a determination to keep the Grammar Schools was electorally popular, Comprehensives were gradually introduced in line with the Crosland plans. Crosland himself was the product of a top public school, Winchester, and his determination to abolish Grammar Schools is curious when set against his preparedness to accept the continuation of the far more socially divisive private sector. The reaction of many middle class parents to comprehensivisation, which might have been anticipated, was a flight into private day schools. Crosland also oversaw a massive expansion of university places. New campuses sprang up on green field sites in the grounds of stately homes on the outskirts of cities like Brighton, Norwich, Lancaster and York, and the country's undergraduate population almost doubled. The Government's intention, and that of Lord Robbins whose recommendations the expansion implemented, was that the beneficiaries should be the working classes, but instead the beneficiaries were women; almost all the new places went to the sisters of the young men who were going to university anyway. The residents of the Diocese of Southwark probably have greater reason to be grateful to the Wilson Government for its decision, implemented in 1969, to establish the University of the Air, later to become known as the Open University, with the inaugural intention of enabling mature people who had missed out first time round to study for a degree.

Another category of school which Crosland left untouched was the Direct Grant Grammar School, a category which included many of the older foundations which had existed prior to 1870. Abolishing these schools was left to a later Labour Government in 1975; the schools were offered the choice either of becoming fully part of the state system, or of joining the private sector, and most of them went private, yet another example of Labour's policies perversely encouraging social divisiveness. This perversity was less in evidence in the Diocese of Southwark than in other places, however, and the diocese's only C of E denominational Direct Grant Grammar School to go private was Emmanuel in Wandsworth. Most of the others bucked the trend and became Comprehensives, but St Saviour's and St Olave's split itself on gender lines; the girls went Comprehensive and stayed in the Old Kent Road, while the boys migrated to Bromley, which still had Grammar Schools because it had formerly been part of Kent, in order to retain their Grammar School status. In 1989 the Inner London Education Authority was abolished, and with it went the myriad of support services, helpful and appreciated though very expensive, which ILEA had provided, and the Inner Boroughs of South London became Education Authorities for the first time. Almost immediately, however, the powers of local education authorities started being whittled away. Kenneth Baker's Education Reform Act of 1988 attempted to devolve power downwards by introducing new arrangements for the local management of schools, and the Governors of Church Schools, most of which had voluntary aided status, found themselves having to assume new and demanding responsibilities. And, since then, the policy of Governments of both colours has been to assume more power for themselves. Numerous directives have been issued requiring the introduction of procedures purportedly aimed at monitoring and therefore improving the quality of educational provision, for example the publication of statistical information, the defining of desirable outcomes and the setting of targets, and the promulgation of league tables. All of this has significantly increased both the administrative workload and also the anxiety and disenchantment of teachers, especially heads, and this anxiety has been compounded by the constant threat of OFSTED inspection.

Each diocese within the Church of England is statutorily required to establish a Diocesan Board for Education to manage its denominational schools, and each Board also has a general responsibility for promoting Christian education throughout its diocesan area. Southwark has ninety-three C of E denominational Primary Schools and fourteen Secondary Schools, and the Secondary Schools include the recently opened St Cecilia's in Wandsworth with its curricular emphasis on music, and the ecumenical St Bede's in Redhill which is a partnership between the Church of England and the Roman Catholic and Nonconformist Churches. The Southwark Board for Education, unlike those of most other dioceses, operates as a free-standing company answerable to the Diocesan Synod rather than as a subcommittee of the Diocesan Board of Finance. In this capacity it hires out its services, in particular supporting the teaching of RE in maintained schools, and it earns almost three quarters of its revenue from this and from other sources, which means that only 28% of its expenses are a demand on diocesan funds. Most of Southwark's C of E schools are voluntary aided, which means that the diocese is responsible for most of what goes on, but a few in the Croydon area which were inherited from the Diocese of Canterbury are voluntary controlled. The Board's policy is to be as inclusive as possible, encouraging the admission of pupils of other faiths and none, and providing for children with a full range of abilities and disabilities; whilst sounding admirable, this policy creates as many problems as it solves, because Church of England schools are generally perceived, including by non-churchgoing parents, as being better than maintained schools, which means that they tend to be oversubscribed, and this in turn means that a number of applications for places, including from churchgoing parents, have to be turned down. Much of the Board's work is concerned with appointing and supporting Governors, with appointing and supporting senior teaching staff, with maintaining the fabric of its school buildings, and with supporting school worship and the teaching of Religious Education. The Board is also statutorily required to collaborate with its constituent local education authorities, and in Southwark this means participating in no less than twelve separate School Organisation Committees, twelve Admissions Forums, twelve Education Policy and Scrutiny Committees, and twelve Standing Advisory Committees for Religious Educations, or SACREs. The responsibility of the SACREs is to draw up and promulgate an agreed syllabus for the teaching of Religious Education throughout the local education authority's schools, and the assumption is that the agreed syllabus will be multi-denominational and multi-faith.

The Southwark Board for Education also supports seven University Chaplains within the diocese. Up till 1992, not counting the Medical Schools, the diocese had only one institution with university status, Goldsmiths' College in New Cross. Goldsmiths was founded in 1891 by the Worshipful Company of Goldsmiths as a "Technical and Recreative Institute", and it became part of the University of London in 1904. In 1977 it absorbed two Teacher Training Colleges, St Gabriel's and Rachel MacMillan, and it became an autonomous college within the University of London in 1988. Then, in 1992, the number of universities within the diocese increased by three. The University of Greenwich started its life in 1890 as the Woolwich Polytechnic, and then absorbed the North West Kent College of Technology in Dartford in 1976, Avery Hill College in 1985, and Garnett College in 1987, and in 1999 moved some of its faculties into its Maritime Campus, part of the former Royal Naval Hospital. The University of the South Bank began in 1891 as the Borough Polytechnic and became the South Bank Polytechnic in 1970, and the University of Kingston grew out of Kingston Polytechnic. In addition to these four there is also King's College which now has its massive Bridgehead Campus south of the river, and the Roehampton University of Surrey which comprises the former Froebel, Whitelands and Southfields Colleges and is part of the University of Surrey Federation. The Board also likes to say that, in addition to its University Chaplains, it also has the "potential" for eleven chaplaincy posts in institutions of Further Education. FE, however, has no formal chaplaincy tradition and there are currently no funds available for the employment of staff, so such work as is done is undertaken by other clergy in their spare time. Most of the diocese's more prestigious private schools also have chaplains, but they are employed by the schools and maintain only minimal links with the Board. One former Diocesan Director of Education, Eric Tinker, was for some of his tenure simultaneously Director of Education for the Diocese of London, and his successors have included Gerald Greenwood and Linda Borthwick.

Youth Work

In 1905 involvement in youth work was a major aspect of South London Church activity, and of the activity of many other overtly Christian organisations like the University and Public School Missions, the YMCA and YWCA, the Church Army, and the Boys' and Girls' Brigades. The Boy Scouts and Girl Guides also had a strongly Christian provenance. Virtually all the young people of the diocese left school at fourteen and virtually all of them continued to live at home, and the churches and other pastoral bodies were quick to recognise that there was an important need for them to be kept profitably occupied and to be helped in the continuation of their education and development. The large Boys' Clubs like Charterhouse and the Bermondsey Boys' Club operated almost as finishing schools for the working classes, and offered a wide range of activities including continuing education and job preparation, and also handicrafts and sport; boxing and football were particularly popular activities, and talent scouts from the Boxing Clubs in the Old Kent Road and from South London's Football League Clubs were regular visitors hunting for potential stars. There were Girls' Clubs too, but their role was less significant because girls were more often kept at home to help with the housework or to mind the younger children. During the twenties and thirties, when unemployment levels were high and young school leavers in particular found it hard to find work, the various youth providers continued to perform an important social role. A high proportion of the young people who left school early were very bright, but they had access to very little money and there were very few other facilities for them to make use of; in particular there were very few opportunities for them to journey outside London, and it was only through their youth work affiliations that they were able to visit the countryside and to do a host of other things that today's young people take for granted. Virtually all youth work was undertaken by volunteers, unpaid and with no professional qualifications except an interest in young people, and working with young people was thought to be a "good thing", particularly by graduates living in the University Settlements. Most parishes had a designated curate with youth work responsibility, and he often exacted a price from his youngsters in the form of compulsory church attendance.

Then came the Second World War. The Blitz and the blackout, and then evacuation, caused the Youth Clubs either to scale down their activities or to close altogether, and the landscape was further changed by the Education Act of 1944. The new Secondary Schools were soon providing a greatly increased range of activities within their own structures, and the widened scope for Grammar School places meant that the brightest children stayed on into the Sixth Form and were kept busy with their academic work. At the same time volunteer youth workers became harder to find; the sort of people who had earlier been willing helpers got married earlier and became busier bringing up their own children, and financial pressures on churches meant that there were fewer curates around to whom youth work responsibility could be delegated. In addition, the ubiquity of National Service created a new demarcation between the world of school and the world of adulthood. The need for change was appreciated in Government, and a Commission was established under the chairmanship of the Countess of Albermarle, whose report, published in 1960, established the Youth Service. The Youth Service was different from what had gone before in two important respects; one was that youth work became professionalised, with nationally agreed salary scales for the employment of trained staff with professional qualifications, and the other was that it became redefined as remedial, or at least preventative. Lady Albermarle's assumption was that the brightest and best young people would have no difficulty in being looked after or in looking after themselves, but that there was a sizable section of young people who were at risk of becoming delinquent, and involvement with the Youth Service would lessen the likelihood of them becoming juvenile offenders. Responsibility for the Youth Service was given to local education authorities which meant that churches, instead of busying themselves with finding volunteer youth workers, had to start busying themselves with making applications for local authority grants so that professional youth workers could be employed. And Albermarle was clairvoyant in anticipating the emergence of the teenager and the teenage culture. During the early 1960s families were becoming a great deal better off, particularly where the mother worked as well as the father, and youngsters who had left school early were able to earn good money without incurring any of the responsibilities on which they might have been required to spend it; it was the era of Bill Haley and the Comets, Teddy Boys, drainpipe trousers, miniskirts and platform shoes. And not only were there commercially based activities in which young people were able to participate, but also the newly emerging advertising industry started focusing its attention on young people and encouraging them to spend their money engaging in these activities. For the most part all this was harmless even if unproductive, but some of it gave rise to public disquiet, particularly when, on a series of Bank Holidays in 1964, much of the youth of South London decamped to the South Coast and trashed Brighton. This reinforced the Albermarle view that there was a hard core of potentially delinquent youth for whom the local education authority funded Youth Service was the panacea. And no local education authority took its Youth Service more seriously than the LCC. Some youth provision was provided directly by the LCC, and later by ILEA, but the authority recognised that much of the expertise lay in the voluntary sector, and in particular with the churches.

The Diocese of Southwark recognised this in appointing, within the structure of its Board for Education, a triumvirate of formidable women to oversee and develop the church's work with children and young people, all three of whom served for more than fifteen years, starting in the mid 1960s and continuing till the early 1980s. They were Margaret Turk who looked after children under 11 and covered Sunday Schools, Eileen Edgar who looked after children between 11 and 14 and covered confirmation classes, and Gwen Rymer who looked after children over 14 and had lead responsibility for delinquent youth. Between them they reckoned to visit every parish every year, and much of the work done by the Diocese of Southwark, funded first by the LCC and later by ILEA, was very imaginative. It gradually spilled over from club-based activities to detached youth work, meeting the young people where they were and getting to know them in coffee bars and on street corners.

"There is no such thing as Society", said Margaret Thatcher soon after arriving in office, and she rode an electoral tide which abandoned the assumption that the richer members of society were socially obliged to pay, through their taxes, to help the rest. Instead she invited her constituency to keep their money and to let the poor look after themselves, and in direct consequence the whole tradition and expertise of youth work eroded and almost collapsed. ILEA itself was wound up and responsibility for education handed over to the boroughs, and the boroughs allocated youth work variously to Leisure Services or to Parks and Amenities and allowed it to slip down the list of priorities. Interest seemed to diminish even within the Southwark Diocesan Board for Education, and in 1992 responsibility for this area of work was handed over to the Area Teams. But since then there has been something of a revival. Lady Albermarle's potential delinquents are now being imaginatively looked after in Exclusion Centres, places set up, often on voluntary sector initiative, for children who have been excluded from school, and where the almost total correlation between exclusion from school, home deprivation, juvenile crime, and drug and alcohol misuse is creatively addressed. And churches too are rediscovering the value of working specifically with young people; there are about fifty youth and children's workers being paid for in parishes, and "Youth for Christ" in Greenwich and "Oxygen" in Kingston are examples of flourishing youth work projects.

Crime and Criminal Justice

South London's reputation for lawlessness developed early, partly because of the area's traditional poverty, and partly because it was easy of access and yet beyond the reach of the authorities of the City; Southwark Cathedral, in its earlier incarnations both as St Mary Overie and as St Saviour's, was a commonly sought sanctuary for criminals fleeing arrest. The area was notorious for prostitution from the Middle Ages up till Victorian times, and in the seventeenth and eighteenth centuries the Vauxhall Pleasure Gardens added to its reputation by offering more elegant but not necessarily more innocent opportunities. Eighteenth century highwaymen found it convenient to stable their horses in St George's Fields, and a *demi-monde* of hangers-on gathered around them and profited from the proceeds of their crimes. Nineteenth century Londoners were fearful of visiting the darkened backstreets of Deptford, Bermondsey and Southwark; the frisson generated by the Jack the Ripper murders may have been particular to the East End, but the stories of Charles Dickens, especially in "Our Mutual Friend", tell of comparably dark deeds and sinister deaths happening south of the river. And the reputation of parts of South London as areas where the arm of the law had difficulty in reaching continued into the twentieth century. Charlie Richardson, South London's equivalent of the Kray twins, grew up in Peckham, and during the 1960s presided over a gangland culture oiled by financial backhanders, and by violence and the threat of violence. He would give those who had crossed him a "bit of a slap", which more often that not resulted in broken bones, and protected himself from prosecution by forging links with people in high places and by bribing the police. He deserved to be brought to justice, but his trial in 1964 broke all the rules of due process. He was nevertheless convicted and sentenced to twenty-five years in prison, of which he served eighteen, though in the middle of his sentence he escaped from high security and fled to Spain, but found he didn't like it, came back and gave himself up, and served out the rest of his time. He is now a successful business man operating on the right side of the law, a rare example of how prison can, on occasion, work. A couple of decades later a comparable culture developed in parts of Brixton, grounded in violence and outwith the rule of law, and based around illegal trafficking in Class A drugs; it brought immunity for some and misery to many, and seriously threatened society as a whole. But South London crime remains, on the whole, remarkable for its pettiness. A scientific study of national importance was carried out in Camberwell and Peckham during the 1960s by Donald West and others which tracked longitudinally a cohort of young boys from deprived backgrounds, and mapped the crimes they committed and their contacts with the police and with the courts. Virtually all the youngsters perpetrated minor delinquencies as juveniles, and then some became habitual adult criminals but most didn't. The most powerful protective factor, in total contradiction to received assumptions, was managing not to get caught; the effect of getting caught and becoming branded as a criminal was shown to exert a far stronger and more lasting influence than any sort of lessons which might have been learned from involvement with the criminal justice system.

A Policeman's Lot, Camberwell Police Station, c 1910

The Bow Street Runners were set up in the 1750s, and the Metropolitan Police in 1829, the first professional police force in the country. The Met was answerable, for want of a better alternative, to the Home Secretary and, anomalously, though there are plans to change things, it still is. Right from the outset the Met's mandate extended south of the river, and the area for which it was responsible expanded as London grew bigger; its boundaries are now roughly coterminous with those of Greater London, though they predate by decades the setting up of the GLC. Surrey Police also has responsibilities within the Diocese of Southwark, covering the Archdeaconry of Reigate. Police organisation changed little during the twentieth century, though police methods continuously developed. There is a constant tension between the demand for "community policing" with bobbies visibly on the beat, and the undercover work which is necessary for addressing more endemic criminality, in South London particularly around trafficking in drugs. What embodied the virtues of neither, however, was the police heavy-handedness which was exemplified in Operation Swamp and which provoked the Brixton riots of 1981 (see page 33). The Scarman Inquiry which followed the riots led to changes in policing methods, but addressing the police's inherent institutional racism had to wait until the Macpherson Inquiry which was set up following the murder of Stephen Lawrence in 1993 (see page 34). Remarkably, there has always been a strong Christian presence within the Metropolitan Police, perhaps most notably in the person of Inspector Barry Wright, an ordained priest who became the diocese's first non-stipendiary canon and later chaplain to the Met (see page 39).

The criminal court system is also a Victorian legacy which changed little during the twentieth century; perhaps the biggest change has been the gradual shift towards a stipendiary magistracy. South London's biggest court complex is the Inner London Sessions Courts in Newington Causeway, and not far away is the Blackfriars Crown Court which used until recently to be called the Marylebone Crown Court in anachronistic commemoration of its origins north of the river. There are also Crown Courts in Woolwich, Southwark, Croydon and Kingston. Associated with the Courts since 1980 has been the Victim Support Scheme which helps the victims of crime and which has its national headquarters in Kennington, and this has been supplemented since 1998 by the Witness Support Scheme which protects and supports witnesses who are at risk of being traumatised or intimidated.

South London has always had its famous prisons; the two best known, both long since gone, were the Clink on Bankside which was under the jurisdiction of the Bishops of Winchester, and the Marshalsea, the debtors' prison in the Borough which provides the setting for Dickens's "Little Dorrit". Today there are Belmarsh, Brixton and Wandsworth, and Latchmere House in Ham. A fact which is not generally appreciated is that the Church of England has a statutory role in prison provision; under the terms of the 1952 Prison Act, and under the terms of the earlier measures which preceded it, a prison cannot exist unless it has a Governor, a Medical Officer, a Board of Visitors (now known as its Independent Monitoring Board), and a Church of England Chaplain. A strong Church presence in prisons dates for the most part from the Evangelical revival of the early nineteenth century, when a prison sentence was seen as a metaphor for the processes of confession, repentance and absolution, and the Prison Service has been permeated ever since by this tension in its purpose between punishment or reform. The Prison Chaplain's traditional role was to encourage repentance, but he also has a statutory responsibility for ensuring that prisoners are treated with the respect that their humanity deserves, and that the prison is managed as a humane institution. The Church of England's statutory role may be difficult to defend now that prisoners are of all faiths and none, but it is nonetheless a privilege which gives the C of E an authority in developing chaplaincy services amongst other denominations and other faiths, and in pioneering methods of pastoral care which make no overt use of Christian jargon. An important protagonist of the Prison Chaplaincy in the Diocese of Southwark was Keith Pound, who went from being Team Rector of Thamesmead to being Chaplain of Brixton, and then became the Chaplain General of the Prison Service, and valuable contributions have also been made by two long-serving chaplains, Philip Meaden at Wandsworth and Patrick Rosheuvel, a Guyanese, at Brixton.

Entertainment

The most widely available entertainment medium in 1905 was the tabloid newspaper. The final years of Queen Victoria's reign had been the heyday of the provincial press, of the Manchester Guardian, the Yorkshire Post and the Western Daily Press, but by the turn of the century, aided by developments in printing technology and improvements in distribution by railway, the London-based nationals had taken centre-stage. The first person to anticipate that national newspapers were capable of attracting a popular readership was Alfred Harmsworth, later Lord Northbrook, who launched the Daily Mail in 1896, insisting that it carry a women's page to complement its sports coverage, and in 1903 he launched a paper aimed exclusively at women, with a title specially designed to attract them, the Daily Mirror; as a women's paper it failed, but he relaunched it a year later as the first national tabloid. Then in 1916 Max Aitken, later Lord Beaverbrook, bought and expanded the Daily Express. Newspaper circulation continued to expand up till its peak year, which was 1936; the circulation of daily newspapers almost equalled the number of families in the country, and that of Sunday newspapers exceeded it. The reason for the subsequent decline was the growing popularity of radio. The BBC was launched in 1922, with the high-minded, puritanical and dictatorial John Reith as its first director-general who, unlike Northbrook and Beaverbrook, saw broadcasting as a vehicle for bringing about "cultural improvement", insisting for example that his announcers speak "standard English". In 1923 the first religious service was broadcast, though from St Martin-in-the-Fields rather than from Southwark Cathedral (see page 81), and in 1927 Reith rescued the ailing Henry Wood Promenade Concerts by transmitting them on the BBC. Reith refused to mix radio with politics, and this alienated Winston Churchill who dismissed him when he became Prime Minister in 1940. The relaxation which followed his departure, however, enabled wartime radio to carry Churchill's celebrated speeches, Vera Lynn singing "We'll Meet Again" on the newly established Forces Network, comedy series like Tommy Handley's ITMA ("It's That Man Again"), and the big dance bands of Henry Hall and Jack Payne.

What people went to for a night out at the turn of the century was the Music Hall. The south bank flagship had earlier been the Old Vic, but it closed in 1880 leaving the field to other popular venues such as the Canterbury Hall near Waterloo Station and the South London and the Surrey near the Elephant and Castle; sadly, all three of these theatres were destroyed by bombing in the 1940s. One of the Surrey's home-grown Music Hall stars, Charlie Chaplin, went off to America to become a legend in a brand new medium, moving pictures. British film-making came into its own in the 1930s, and when the war came Churchill was quick to appreciate its potential for morale-raising propaganda, personally encouraging the making of films like "In Which We Serve" (1942) and Laurence Olivier's "Henry V" (1944). During the 1950s, however, high seriousness gave place to the Ealing comedies, a remarkable number of them with South London settings, for example "The Lavender Hill Mob" (1951) and "The Lady Killers" (1955); "Passport to Pimlico" (1949), even though nominally set north of the river, has a South London ambience and was filmed amongst the terraced houses that were about to be demolished prior to the construction of the Lambeth Walk Estate. South London's 1950s hero, or anti-hero, on radio, film and television, was Tony Hancock, who allegedly lived at Railway Cuttings, East Cheam, and later multi-media celebrities who lived allegedly within the diocese included the Wombles of Wimbledon Common. Post-Ealing movies with a South London setting include Antonioni's "Blow Up" (1966), filmed in Maryon Park in Charlton where it is commemorated by a plaque, "My Beautiful Launderette" (1985), "The End of the Affair" (2002), and "Charlie" (2003) which depicted the life and troublesome times of Charlie Richardson (see page 61).

The cinema's peak year was 1949 when attendance was 1.6 billion, implying that every British adult went to the cinema almost once a week, but by 1956 this figure had dropped to a third and by 1962 to a quarter. In the same way that radio displaced newspapers, the cinema was displaced by television. The BBC had pioneered television during the late 1930s but had decided not to develop it because of the war, and an indication of the Corporation's priorities was the decision of William Haley, Reith's successor, to keep his offices in Broadcasting House. What gave television lift-off was its coverage of Queen Elizabeth II's coronation, and the number of television licences increased fivefold between 1950 and 1955. For a number of years the reverent tones of Richard Dimbleby and the earnestness of "Watch with Mother" reflected the earlier high-mindedness of Lord Reith, but in 1954 the Government bowed to commercial pressure and allowed the advent of a rival channel funded by advertising. For a while ITV aped the seriousness of the BBC but, under pressure from the advertisers to increase its audience ratings, it moved down-market and its viewing figures equalled and then passed those of the BBC. The BBC, seeking to justify its licence fee, sought to recapture the initiative and dumbing down began, a process that was accelerated by the introduction of analogue and then digital and the subsequent proliferation of channels; satellite dishes now make their own special contribution to the complexity of the South London skyline.

The most celebrated nineteenth century novel with a South London setting is Dickens's "Little Dorrit" which happens in the Marshalsea Prison and in the Church of St George the Martyr, and it is interesting that Becky Sharp, the heroine of Thackeray's "Vanity Fair", lived in Camberwell in the days when it was a fashionable address. The development of South London's suburbia was chronicled both by G.K.Chesterton, whose "Napoleon of Notting Hill" (1904) satirises the pretentiousness of local government, with Wimbledon building its own city walls and Surbiton instituting a morning bell to rouse its citizens for work, and by H.G.Wells, particularly in "Tono Bungay" and "Ann Veronica", both published in 1905. Since then, however, novels with a South London setting seem sadly to have been few and far between; the few that spring to mind include Graham Greene's "The End of the Affair" (1951), Muriel Spark's "The Ballad of Peckham Rye" (1960), Hanif Kureishi's "The Buddha of Suburbia" (1990), and Margaret Forster's "Diary of an Ordinary Woman" (2003).

In the world of theatre, however, South London has happily achieved a greater eminence. The Old Vic's closure as a Music Hall in 1880 was a consequence of the prudish altruism of Emma Cons, who bought it and turned it into a "cheap and decent place of amusement on strict temperance lines"; her name is now commemorated in a rather drab little garden opposite the theatre. She died in 1912 and bequeathed it to her niece Lilian Baylis, more high-browed but less high-minded than her aunt, and a worshipper at St Paul's Lorrimore Square. She used her inheritance to make genuine drama available to a mass audience; admission to a wooden seat up in the Old Vic gods cost sixpence. She later passed the management successively to two of Theatre's early knights, Tyrone Guthrie and John Gielgud, and between 1953 and 1958 an ambitious "five year plan" was launched which memorably staged every single one of Shakespeare's plays. In 1963 yet another knight, who later became Theatre's first Lord, Laurence Olivier, took his newly formed National Theatre Company there, appropriately enough since up till then the Old Vic had been the country's national theatre in all but name. The company performed there, with barely an empty seat in the house, until 1976 when Denys Lasdun's building on the South Bank was at long last ready. The Young Vic opened on the opposite side of the road in 1970, and a more ambitious project was Sam Wanamaker's dream of constructing a replica, almost on its original site, of Shakespeare's Globe; sadly he died in 1993 and did not live to see his theatre's opening performance in April 1997, though it was attended by his actress daughter Zoe. Other theatres in the diocese include the Greenwich, the Battersea Arts Centre, the Ashcroft and the Warehouse in Croydon, the Wimbledon, and the Royal and the Orange Tree in Richmond, and these will soon be joined by the new Rose in Kingston. The National Theatre became Royal in 1988, having earlier staged David Hare's "Racing Demon", a memorable but none too flattering picture of the Church in South London with fictional Bishops of Southwark and of Kingston as its leading villains. For most of its life the National has had its own chaplain, the first being Eric Mathieson, Vicar of St Alphege Southwark and himself an actor and a playwright, who famously participated in a revival of the Mystery Plays as the leading sinner, which required him to be consigned nightly to the fires of hell whilst wearing his own dog collar. The diocese's top *alma mater* for dramatists would seem to be Kingston Grammar School, which has produced

Globes, New and Old, today and 1616

R.C.Sherriff who wrote *inter alia* the First World War classic "Journey's End", and Michael Frayn, author of such various fare as "Noises Off", "Copenhagen" and more recently "Democracy".

The Diocese of Southwark played host to the twentieth century's two most important national exhibitions, the Festival of Britain in 1951 and the Millennium Experience in 2000, and it also gave house room to the discarded residue of the nineteenth century's biggest and best, the Great Exhibition of 1851. The Crystal Palace which had housed the Great Exhibition was assembled in Hyde Park in only three months using prefabricated sections, and the Exhibition itself was phenomenally successful. Prince Albert sponsored it, Queen Victoria enthused about it, and it was visited by more than six million people including a well-behaved party from Lingfield in Surrey (see page 3). The huge profits which it generated were used to build and endow the Albert Hall, the Victoria and Albert Museum, the Natural History Museum and the Science Museum, and its building became so popular that, instead of it being demolished as had initially been intended, it was dismantled and reassembled south of the river. There it remained for more than eighty years, a prominent landmark for the Diocese of Southwark's early inhabitants, and a Sunday afternoon attraction which was visited by many. Then, in 1936, providing the diocese with one of its biggest ever spectacles, it burned down, perhaps a fitting end for a building which had outlived its usefulness and become worn out and tawdry. All that remains apart from its foundations are a number of life-sized plaster dinosaurs, though it has given its name to a park, a railway station and a professional football club and, even after its demise, to a national athletics stadium and to Southern England's first Olympic sized swimming pool.

The Great Exhibition was successful because it looked to the future, offering the promise of an improvement in living standards through the application of technology, and on this promise it largely delivered. The Festival of Britain, planned ostensibly to celebrate the Great Exhibition's centenary but in fact to mark the ending of post-war austerity, was successful largely because it looked to the past, attempting to promise the restoration of the Britain which World War II had interrupted. It was set in several acres of derelict dockland between Waterloo Station and the river, and its features included the Dome of Discovery and the Skylon, a suspended illuminated shaft; Southwark Cathedral contributed by staging a musical Passion Play. The only one of its original buildings which still remains is the Royal Festival Hall, designed by Leslie Martin of the LCC Architects Department; plans were made at the time for the Festival Hall's later expansion, and Martin later designed the Queen Elizabeth Hall, the Purcell Room and the Hayward Gallery which were opened between 1965 and 1968. Other art galleries within the diocese include The Dulwich Picture Gallery, founded in 1811 to house paintings which had been surreptitiously purchased by agents working for King Stanislaus Augustus to form a national collection for Poland, but which had been rendered otiose by Poland's disappearance from Europe's map in 1795, and Tate Modern which was created from the shell of the Bankside power station to celebrate the millennium. The initial intention for the Festival of Britain site was that it should also include a National Theatre. An enabling Act of Parliament was passed in 1949 and a foundation stone laid in 1951, but the project was abandoned in 1961. In 1967, however, this retrograde decision was reversed, and the theatre, designed by Denys Lasdun, was opened in 1976, though quite a distance away from its earlier foundation stone. On the lasting value of the Millennium Experience the jury is still out, though the positives already outweigh the negatives (see page 27), and the Dome, perhaps more interesting architecturally than the Festival Hall, is being refurbished as a music and sports arena which features in London's bid for the 2012 Olympics.

During the first half of the twentieth century one of the sports in which South London excelled was boxing, and its most celebrated venue, until it was destroyed by bombing in 1940, was The Ring in the Blackfriars Road. The Ring was unusual in two respects; it was a converted Nonconformist chapel, and it was managed for most of its thirty year history by a woman, the formidable Bella Burge, who by all accounts would have been capable of taking on most of her contenders. Her policy was to keep admission prices low so that local people could afford to come and watch, but her visitors included, on several recorded occasions, the Prince of Wales who briefly became Edward VIII. The most popular spectator sport, however, then as now, was football, and throughout its hundred year history the Diocese of Southwark has been represented in the Football League by two clubs, Charlton Athletic and Crystal Palace, both of them founded in the same year as the diocese. And it has also gained two and lost two. Millwall crossed the river from the Isle of Dogs to New Cross in 1910, and Woolwich Arsenal departed in the opposite direction *en route* for Highbury in 1913, and Wimbledon came and went. Wimbledon FC started its life as the Old Boys' team from the Central School, was admitted to the Football League in 1977, lost its ground in Plough Lane in 1991, and decamped to Milton Keynes in 2003. No South London team, not even Arsenal while based in Woolwich, has ever won the League, but Wimbledon surprised even its own supporters by winning the FA Cup in 1988, and Charlton had won it earlier in 1947 after losing in the Final the year before. Crystal Palace were the losing finalists in 1990, and so, amazingly, were Millwall in 2004, but on both occasions the ecstatic triumph of having actually got there did much to compensate for the disappointment of eventual defeat. Despite twice visiting Wembley during the 1940s, Charlton does not hold the South London record for Cup Final appearances; a fact known only to dedicated football archivists is that the proud holders of this honour are Clapham Rovers, who won the Cup in 1880 after twice being defeated in the Final. South London has, in fact, hosted the Cup Final more often than it has been represented in it; it was played at the Kennington Oval from 1874 till 1892 and at Crystal Palace from 1895 till 1914. The Kennington Oval is, of course, more celebrated as a cricket ground, the stately home of the Surrey County Cricket Club, which has won the County Championship no less than eighteen times, more often than any other team except Yorkshire, including eleven times since World War II to Yorkshire's eight. The Oval is also a venue for Test Matches, and traditionally plays host to the final Test of each series, most notably in 1953 when Hutton and Compton regained the Ashes for England, and in 1963 when England lost a home series for the first time to the West Indies, though this match was watched by so many South Londoners of Caribbean provenance that it was described at the time as being a home game for the visitors. There are two other world famous sporting venues within the diocese, the athletics ground at Crystal Palace and the home of the All England Lawn Tennis and Croquet Club at Wimbledon, where croquet now takes second place to Grand Slam tennis. The diocese also hosts the start of the annual London Marathon; over thirty thousand runners, some dressed variously as teddy bears or brides and bridegrooms, congregate every April on Blackheath, and then run a semicircular course through Woolwich and Greenwich before disappearing over Tower Bridge on their way towards the finishing line in St James's Park.

SECTION THREE:
THE CHURCH IN SOUTHWARK
Southwark in Winchester, St Mary Overie 750-1540

Unlike the Diocese of London which is very old, allegedly founded in 604, but which has a relatively modern cathedral, the Diocese of Southwark is relatively new but has a very old cathedral. St Mary Overie means St Mary-over-the-River, though the name may derive from a lady called Mary Overy who was one of the church's first benefactresses. The earliest evidence of a religious settlement on the present cathedral's site dates from the seventh century, the heyday of Saxon Christianity. The Roman London Bridge had long since collapsed and been replaced by a ferry crossing, and churches were built at both its ends, St Magnus the Martyr on the north bank and St Mary Overie on the south. A little later Bishop Justus of Rochester, one of the dignitaries whose effigy now graces the cathedral's altar screen, founded a couple of nunneries, one at St Mary Overie and the other in Chertsey. Then, in the ninth century, England was invaded by the Danes. The Danes captured most of the north and the east of the country, but the Saxons fought back under King Alfred and held onto most of the south and the west. St Swithun, King Alfred's Bishop of Winchester and another of the dignitaries on the altar screen, rebuilt London Bridge and annexed St Mary Overie for his own diocese. He died at St Mary's, and efforts to transport his body back to Winchester were thwarted, so the nursery rhyme says, by forty days of rain. In 1012 the Danes invaded again, and this time managed to capture both London and the South Bank settlement, the Suthvirk. The Saxon King Ethelred the Unready determined to win them both back again, and enlisted for this purpose an unlikely ally in King Olaf of Norway. Olaf's strategy was to isolate London from its Suthvirk, and in order to do this he had first to destroy St Swithun's bridge. He managed this by fastening tow ropes to the bridge's wooden supports, and getting his strong Norwegian oarsmen to pull them apart; "London Bridge is falling down", sang the delighted Saxons as they watched, giving rise as they did so to the second nursery rhyme to have originated in St Mary Overie's churchyard within two hundred years.

The Vischer Panorama of 1616, showing from left to right,
Winchester House, St Mary Overie, London Bridge and St Olave's

Olaf succeeded in capturing first the Suthvirk and then London; he then converted to Christianity, and in return was canonised and later commemorated both by the Church of St Olave's, built just downstream from St Mary's, and also by yet another effigy on the altar screen.

After the Norman Conquest a Cluniac monastery was founded in Bermondsey, and St Mary Overie became a priory staffed by a team of canons dedicated to working amongst the poor people of Southwark and to looking after the travellers crossing the rebuilt bridge. The Norman and Mediaeval Bishops of Winchester were powerful politicians as well as senior prelates, and Bishop William Giffard in the twelfth century built himself a palace just upstream from St Mary's which became known as Winchester House. From it he exercised both ecclesiastical and secular justice, and he found it necessary to build his own prison which became known as "The Clink". After the murder of Thomas a Becket in 1170 the canons of St Mary Overie dedicated their hospice to their new saint, and the original site of St Thomas's Hospital was very close to the church in what is still called St Thomas's Street. Giffard's successors as powerful Bishops of Winchester included Peter des Roches during the reigns of King John and Richard I who rebuilt St Mary Overie in very much the form in which it exists today, and William of Wykeham during the reigns of Edward III and Richard II who continued Peter des Roches's building programmes both at St Mary's and at Winchester House. William of Wykeham also saw off the Peasants' Revolt, the first of a succession of rebellions which originated in Kent and passed through, or attempted to pass through, St Mary's churchyard with revolutionary intent; Wat Tyler and his rebels assembled on Blackheath in 1381 where they listened to a famous sermon by John Ball, an early Christian Socialist priest, and then proceeded to Southwark where they caused mayhem before successfully crossing London Bridge only to be deceived by the young King Richard II who pretended to parley with them in Finsbury Fields. Later in Richard II's reign the poet Geoffrey Chaucer crossed the bridge in the opposite direction in the company of his band of pilgrims bound for Canterbury, and they spent their first night at the Tabard in what is now Borough High Street. More relevant to the history of St Mary Overie, however, was the residence there as one of its canons, from 1380 till his death in 1408, of the poet John Gower.

In the same mould as Peter des Roches and William of Wykeham was Henry Beaufort, Bishop of Winchester during the reigns of Henrys IV, V and VI. Beaufort was a loyal supporter of the usurper Henry IV, and later he blessed the young King Henry V as he passed through Southwark on his way to fight the Battle of Agincourt. Later still Beaufort raised a crusading army to fight against the Hussite heretics in Bohemia, but he diverted them instead to fight unsuccessfully in France against Joan of Arc; he appears as a major character in Shakespeare's Henry VI play cycle. He also presided, in St Mary Overie, at two royal weddings. The first was in 1406 when he married the Earl of Kent to Lucia of Milan, but the Earl died only a year later in a naval battle off Brittany; his widow remained in England, and used her inheritance to fund the building of Milan's new cathedral, creating its unlikely link with the Cathedral Church of Southwark. The other was in 1423 between his own niece Joan and King James I of Scotland; James had been captured by the English as a young lad and held hostage for eighteen years, but Beaufort had brought him up as his own son. Perhaps the best poetry written by a reigning monarch is the long love poem "King's Quair" which James wrote to his wife, but tragically both King and Queen were murdered side by side in a rebellion of Scottish noblemen in 1437. Beaufort's successor as Bishop of Winchester was William Wainfleet, who attempted to negotiate a peaceful resolution to yet another Kentish rebellion, this one led by Jack Cade in 1452, when the churchyard was again the scene of bloody fighting. Despite this and several other violent interludes, Southwark during the Middle Ages was an area of economic bustle with itinerant travellers being serviced by the vendors of the Borough Market, and in the middle of it all the peaceful and tranquil haven of the priory.

Southwark in Winchester, St Saviour's 1540-1877

There are records of a chapter convention held in Leicester in 1518 of the priors of all the Augustinian houses in England. St Mary Overie was represented by Prior Bartholomew Linstead, who made an impassioned plea for stricter observance of the monastic rule and for a deeper spirituality, both of which embarrassed the more worldly priors from elsewhere. Linstead nevertheless had his way in Southwark, and for more than thirty years was allowed to run his house in the manner to which he aspired. But then, in 1540, Henry VIII dissolved the monasteries. Two of the dissolved monasteries in South London, Bermondsey and Merton, have disappeared almost without trace; Bermondsey Abbey is at least commemorated by a road named Abbey Street which marks the site of its nave, but the site of Merton Abbey is now a railway siding. St Mary Overie managed to survive by becoming a parish church and by changing its dedication. Prior Linstead negotiated the deconsecration and demolition of the nearby church of St Margaret's and the transfer of its parochial function to St Mary's, which was renamed St Saviour's. He and the twelve remaining canons received a pension, and for this he was unfairly excoriated by the diarist Aubrey for having sold out. Because of its antecedents as a priory, St Saviour's became an unusual parish church; it was owned directly by its parishioners who ran it and raised money for its upkeep through a large body known as the vestrymen, and its incumbent, who had no tenure, was known as the chaplain. To begin with, there was nowhere for the chaplain to live.

Henry VIII's decision to dissolve the monasteries was an important step in England becoming a Protestant nation, but Stephen Gardiner, the Bishop of Winchester who oversaw the dissolution in South London, was an extreme Catholic and his episcopacy was marked by denominational strife. First he uncovered a cell of Protestant extremists who had printed an English translation of the Bible using the presses of St Thomas's

Hospital, and this led to burnings for heresy in front of the newly built church of St George's on Borough High Street. Gardiner then, because of his Catholic leanings, spent most of Edward VI's reign depossessed and imprisoned in the Tower, but he was later released by the Catholic Queen Mary who reinstated him as Bishop of Winchester. He rewarded her by hosting at Winchester House the negotiations that led to her marriage to Philip II of Spain, but this then meant that he became the target of xenophobic unpopularity caused first by the Spanish alliance, and then by his role in the suppression of Sir Thomas Wyatt's Protestant rebellion; Gardiner prevented Wyatt's Kentishmen from crossing London Bridge, and arranged for the guns of the Tower to be trained on the churches of St Olave's and St Saviour's which the rebels had occupied. Wyatt, however, blinked first, and led his army round by the nearest alternative river crossing which was at Kingston, and this dissipated the momentum of his rebellion. In 1554 Gardiner presided first over the informal examinations at Winchester House of the seven Protestant churchmen who had refused to accept Mary's Catholicism, and then over their formal trials in the north transept of St Saviour's Church. All seven, including John Hooper the former Bishop of Gloucester, were burned at the stake. Gardiner died in 1555, the last of Winchester's Catholic bishops, and his coffin was carried in a lavish procession from Southwark to Winchester Cathedral.

In Queen Elizabeth I's reign the character of the South Bank changed radically. The centre of gravity north of the river shifted westwards, and living in Southwark ceased being convenient for the great and the good. The grander palaces, including Winchester House, fell into decay and were divided up into tenements, and Bankside resumed its role as London's red light district. But, as well as housing London's brothels, it also housed its theatres, the Rose, the Swan, and later the great Globe itself. Philip Henslowe and Edward Alleyn, the father- and son-in-law team who were the great impresarios of the Elizabethan theatre, were both vestrymen of St Saviour's, and they played an active part in an important development for St Saviour's, the securing of a parsonage. Alleyn later moved to Dulwich where he founded Dulwich College, or "The College of God's Gift" as it was initially known, but Henslowe remained in St Saviour's parish till his death in 1616. Despite the cathedral's monument to Shakespeare there is no record of the bard ever having worshipped at St Saviour's, but other theatrical names who are known to have done so include Francis Beaumont, John Fletcher and Philip Massinger.

The congregation of St Saviour's between the death of Queen Elizabeth I and the outbreak of the Civil War was socially mixed. The area south of the church, already known by then as "The Borough", was being developed as a respectable area for London's solider citizens who commuted across the Bridge, and during services they rubbed shoulders with the inhabitants of the Bankside "stews" and with travellers who were passing through. The Elizabethan Poor Law system placed on parishes the responsibility for caring for the poor and needy, and this gave them a strong but shameful incentive to employ marshals to move vagrants on, especially women. The reports of Marshal Christopher Fawcett in 1622 make sad reading; he says that he heard that "Mary Moore and a child with her were lying very sick at St Margaret's Hill, being come out of St George's Parish", but he "got her and her child carried back again to St George's, and so was rid of her", and that "having heard that Elizabeth Rogers, being great with child and in pain of childbirth, coming from the other side of London and sat at the new churchyard, I went presently to her and with much ado got her over the bridge and so heard no more of her". Nevertheless, a great deal of charitable work was done. St Saviour's founded a Grammar School in 1562, and St Olave's did the same in 1571. Thomas Cure founded his almshouses in 1579 which later relocated to

Norwood, and two John Marshalls, father and son, established a charity in the 1620s which to this day is a major source of funding for worthwhile projects in the locality. But perhaps the most remarkable charitable endowment during these years happened on the other side of the Atlantic. Robert Harvard was a vestryman of St Saviour's who had played a major role in the good works of the early seventeenth century, but he and most of his family died in the plague of 1625 and his widow and young son John then left the parish. John later went to Emmanuel College Cambridge, and later still emigrated to Massachusetts. His aspiration was to found a university in the New World, and he nostalgically renamed as Cambridge the suburb of Boston in which it was to be located. When he died in 1638, he divided his fortune equally between St Saviour's Church and the newly founded university which continues to bear his name.

The Bishop of Winchester during most of James I's reign was the saintly High Churchman Lancelot Andrewes, the last episcopal occupant of Winchester House. During his tenure the seeds of Dissent were beginning to germinate, not just in worship but also in the sympathies of those who exercised secular authority. In 1621 a group of Anabaptists started meeting in a house in Deadman's Place, literally under St Saviour's shadow, and in 1640 they were apprehended by the marshal and removed to the Clink; the local magistrates, however, were sympathetic to their cause, and all that happened was they were reprimanded and released. Anabaptist assemblies were particularly prevalent in St Olave's parish with its large contingent of foreign immigrants, particularly from the Netherlands, and the most notable sermons in the area were being preached, not in any of the Anglican churches, but in the open air or in the new Independent Meeting House in Deadman's Lane by the likes of John Bunyan and Richard Baxter; no action was taken to move these illegal worshippers on. In 1641 a group of Dissenters broke into St Saviour's during a service and pulled down and destroyed the communion rails; the magistrates ordered the rails to be replaced, but nothing happened because the culprits were too poor to meet the cost. Similar disturbances happened at St Olave's and at St George's.

Though the southern bank of the Thames was one of the areas where Dissent was strongest, the policy of Charles I throughout most of his reign was to attempt to suppress it. One group of Dissenters decided that flight was their best option, and in 1620 they set sail from Rotherhithe, bound first for Amsterdam and then for Massachusetts. Their departure is commemorated by a plaque, by a statue on the Thames Path, by a United Reformed Church which is now sadly closed, and by a pub on the riverbank; the pub, named after the boat in which they sailed, is called the Mayflower. Once the Civil War had started, London became a Parliamentary stronghold, though Southwark's churches were less than sympathetic to its cause. In November 1642 Parliament called for an enforced loan from all London parishes, and the vestrymen of St Saviour's contributed only £98, a paltry sum when compared with £11,000 donated by St Lawrence Jewry on the other side of the river. The clergy at St Olave's and St George's were replaced, but somehow those at St Saviour's managed to remain in office and the Grammar School continued to function. Winchester House, bereft of its bishop who had fled the capital, was used as a prison, and its inmates included the pamphleteer John Lilburne of whom it was said that "he would argue with himself if there were no one else to argue with him". The theatres on Bankside were all closed, the Globe in 1644, and marriages started being conducted by magistrates rather than clergy. Parishes became units in an early form of local democracy, and St Saviour's became just "Saviour's" because the word "saint" had been proscribed for other uses. And there were real privations too, with the Royalist Navy blockading the mouth of the Thames so that coal from Newcastle couldn't get through.

The Restoration brought back the Stuart monarchy but failed to restore to Southwark any of its former glory. The grand houses had all been abandoned, and when the theatres reopened it was in Drury Lane and Covent Garden and not on Bankside. Southwark regained its reputation for lawlessness and prostitution, and the recorded crossings of London Bridge by Samuel Pepys were all with solely licentious intent. Winchester House had deteriorated during its time as a Commonwealth prison to such an extent that it was never restored, and St Saviour's thus lost its neighbourly link with its bishops. And St Saviour's also lost the more prosperous half of its congregation when the John Marshall legacy was used to build the new Christchurch in 1671. The Great Fire of London in 1666 caused a rush of refugees to seek shelter in the church and its churchyard, but in 1675 the South Bank had a great fire of its own which gutted the whole of the Borough and necessitated the blowing up of houses in the neighbourhood of St Saviour's as part of an attempt, in the event successful, to save the church itself from burning down.

Thomas Guy, a local bookseller who had invested in the South Sea Bubble but had managed to get his money out before the bubble burst, died in 1724. He had been worried during his lifetime by the extent to which St Thomas's Hospital had become too small to accommodate the locality's sick, so he used his accumulated wealth to endow another hospital on the opposite side of the street. From then on Guy's eclipsed St Thomas's until the latter moved to Lambeth in 1862 (see page 48). In 1738 the church of St George the Martyr was rebuilt in its present form, and stole yet more rich parishioners away from St Saviour's. The two most celebrated Chaplains of St Saviour's during the eighteenth century were memorable not so much for their ministry as for the trouble that they caused. Dr Henry Sacheverell was appointed in 1710, but before taking up his appointment he preached two sermons which were so virulently High Church Tory that the Whig Government impeached him. He was convicted in the Court of Arches and banned from preaching for three years, but his punishment enhanced rather than diminished his reputation, and St Saviour's became a place of pilgrimage for people who wanted to look at the Doctor even though they weren't able to hear him preach. And then, during the latter half of the century, the Chaplain Thomas Jones got into trouble because of his Evangelical enthusiasm, which again attracted a wide audience; he later left the mainstream Church of England to join John Wesley's Methodist movement. During the period of calm between the tenure of these two chaplains one of the St Saviour's vestryman was Ralph Thrale, the owner of a large brewery in Southwark and the husband of Hester who played hostess to the *literati* of her day, including Dr Samuel Johnson and James Boswell. The brewery gained its place in history during the Gordon Riots of 1780 when a mob that had assembled on St George's Fields to protest against the relaxation of the laws against Roman Catholics was diverted from hostility by offers of beer; the rioters, almost in passing, burned down the Clink, and from then on it was never again used as a prison, though its name has a continuing usage in the criminal vocabulary. One of history's ironies is that the place where Lord George Gordon called together his anti-Catholic rioters is now the site of St George's Roman Catholic Cathedral. The Catholic Emancipation Act of 1829 ended most of the anti-Catholic discrimination, and St George's was consecrated as a church in 1848. England's Roman Catholic episcopal hierarchy was restored in 1850, and St George's became the country's first Roman Catholic cathedral since the Reformation with Thomas Grant installed the following year as the first Bishop of Southwark, more than half a century before his first Anglican counterpart. The building was destroyed by bombing in 1941, and reopened after major refurbishment in 1958.

In 1827 Charles Sumner became Bishop of Winchester, the first of a generation of reforming Evangelical bishops who transformed the Church of England. During the course of his long episcopacy St Saviour's suffered three diminutions, two to the churchyard and one to the nave. The authorities of the City of London had decided that London Bridge had become an inadequate thoroughfare for the increasing quantity of traffic crossing the river, and that it needed replacing. They commissioned the architect James Rennie to build the new bridge, and specified that he should do so a few yards upstream from the existing bridge in order to allow it to remain open till the new one was up and running. Work started in 1825, but the new bridge required a new approach road, and the new approach road, unaltered to the present day, required the building of a retaining wall right across St Saviour's churchyard, coming almost up to the church itself. Protests were lodged, but unsurprisingly they cut little ice with the City authorities. The Mediaeval Bishop's Chapel had to be demolished and there was even talk of demolishing the Lady Chapel, the Church's easternmost and oldest part, but in the event the Lady Chapel managed to survive though with very little space between it and the approach road's embankment. Then, in 1836, came the London Chatham and Dover Railway and the opening of London Bridge Station. This required the building of a viaduct across the southern side of the churchyard, also still in existence, separating it off from the Borough Market and reducing yet further the churchyard's size and spaciousness. And then, in 1841, the Mediaeval nave was pulled down. Financial responsibility for the upkeep of the church had been vested, ever since the Reformation, in the parishioners, and the parishioners' only source of income was the rates. Rates were very unpopular since they were a charge on all the inhabitants of the parish irrespective of whether or not they chose to come to church, and were also a political issue in that they had to be paid by non-Anglicans who received no benefit for their outlay. Repairing the nave was presented as an expensive option, and a rebuild as very much cheaper. There was some protest from the conservationist lobby, in particular from the High Church theologian and harbinger of the Oxford Movement F.D.Maurice who was then working at Guy's, and also from that perpetual proponent of the ineffability of all things Gothic, the architect Pugin who was later to rebuild the Houses of Parliament. The parsimonious vestrymen, however, had their way. Their replacement nave was by all accounts both ugly and shoddy, and its only virtue was that it lasted less then fifty years. Nevertheless, despite all these privations, and despite the increase in the parish's population and poverty, the pastoral work of the church continued, in particular through the long ministry of Samuel Benson, first as curate and then as chaplain.

Southwark in Rochester 1877-1905, and Bishop Edward Talbot 1905-1911

When Queen Victoria came to the throne in 1837, the diocesan structure of the Church of England was still much the same as it had been during the Middle Ages; the only new diocese to have been created since the Reformation was Ripon in 1836 to accommodate the burgeoning city of Leeds. Small rural dioceses like Hereford existed alongside vast conglomerates like Chester which included both Manchester and Liverpool and extended up as far as the Lake District, Worcester which included Birmingham, and Lincoln which stretched as far south as Leicester. And, of these conglomerate dioceses, perhaps the oddest was Rochester which included most of Hertfordshire and Essex. It was clear that most of these Mediaeval dioceses had become too large given the vast increases in population, and that they were inappropriately configured given the enormous demographic shifts that had taken place. A first step towards rationalisation was taken in 1877 when two new dioceses were created, Truro which was carved out of Exeter, and St Albans which was carved out of Rochester with a little bit of London thrown in. But the creation of the Diocese of St Albans had consequences in that the Diocese of Rochester was "compensated" for the loss of Hertfordshire by being given, for reasons which now seem almost impossible to understand, the whole of South London and a significant chunk of Surrey which had previously been part of another unmanageable conglomerate, Winchester. This arrangement was never popular because a great many Anglicans in South London were already cherishing aspirations for becoming a diocese in their own right, and because Surrey resented becoming part of a diocese based in Kent.

The first Bishop of the newly constituted Diocese of Rochester was Anthony Thorold, an Evangelical disciplinarian whose appointment was disliked by the Church's Anglo-Catholic wing. He complained to the Home Secretary that his new diocese was too awkward to manage, not least because it wasn't even in one piece since South London was separated from the Medway Towns by a sliver of Canterbury which included Sevenoaks and Orpington and touched the Thames at Erith. But he was told that the decision had been made, and that he had to put up with it and get on with the job. As well as this, the problems of South London were enormous and becoming well publicised; it was during Thorold's episcopacy that Charles Booth described the South London riverside as "the world's longest stretch of unbroken poverty", and public anxiety was everywhere being expressed about the ungodliness of the poor people's behaviour. And another problem was the poverty of the Church; Rochester had never been a particularly rich diocese, and Thorold was only too well aware that any revival of the Church in South London was going to require a great deal of money for which there was no obvious source. A philanthropist who did as much as anyone to ameliorate the area's poverty was Octavia Hill, who came to London from Cambridgeshire in 1852 and was one of the early Christian Socialists alongside F.D.Maurice. Her most significant contribution was in the field of housing management; with the help of John Ruskin, who then lived in Herne Hill, she bought up a number of houses in South London and managed their maintenance and letting so efficiently that she was able to pay an annual dividend of 5% to her investors, and so humanely that she was asked by the Ecclesiastical Commissioners in 1884 to take over responsibility for their entire property portfolio in Southwark, especially around St Peter's Walworth and St John's Waterloo. During her spare moments she was instrumental in founding the Charity Organisation Society and the National Trust, and the evidence that she provided for the Royal Commission on the Aged Poor in 1893 anticipated the Old Age Pension. She died in 1902, and her Memorial Service was held at St Saviour's.

Despite all the difficulties which confronted him, Thorold actually managed to achieve a great deal. Although he had earlier been such an extreme Evangelical that he had refused even to enter Anglo-Catholic churches, he assumed an irenic position and did much to heal the rift between the Church's rival wings. He set the tone for his episcopacy during the first year of his appointment when he came to the rescue of a vicar in Hatcham whose practices had been publicised as being a little too close to Rome, and whose church was under physical attack from gangs of dockers who had been paid by the Evangelical lobby to break it up. Thorold took an active interest in the work of the diocese's parochial schools, and oversaw the foundation of two Teacher Training Colleges, St John's in Battersea for men, and St Gabriel's in Kennington for women; St John's later amalgamated with St Mark's in Chelsea to become "Marjohns" and emigrated to Plymouth in 1973, and St Gabriel's was subsumed within Goldsmiths' in

1977. He was the first Bishop to revive the ancient but long-defunct Order of Deaconesses, inviting Isabella Gilmore to become its first head; she was a former matron at Guy's and the sister of William Morris. The deaconesses were initially housed in Clapham, but later moved their base to Greyladies in Blackheath. And another of Thorold's initiatives which is still very much in evidence today was the link that he established between South London and the University of Cambridge. The first University Settlement had been Toynbee Hall in Stepney, and several Oxford Colleges had followed it with missions to various parts of the East End. Thorold saw South London as an obvious arena for Cambridge competition, and the first College to establish a mission, in Walworth, was St John's; it was named Lady Margaret Settlement after Lady Margaret Beaufort, the mother of the Tudor dynasty and of King Henry VII, who had her own links with South London as a Bishop of Winchester's niece, and had founded St John's in her old age. Corpus Christi then set up an open air Mission under a railway arch in the Borough, Trinity assumed responsibility for the parish of St George's Camberwell, and other missions were founded by Queens', Clare, and Pembroke respectively in Peckham, Rotherhithe, and another part of Walworth. Thorold was adamant that these links should be, as in fact they became, reciprocal; "If Cambridge helps South London", he said, "then South London equally helps Cambridge". Public School missions soon followed, in particular those of Charterhouse, Lancing, Cranleigh, Wellington and Cheltenham, and also the United Girls' Schools Mission at St Mark's Camberwell. Cambridge House, a residential settlement engaged in a broader spectrum of pastoral work, was founded in Camberwell in 1889.

Thorold's most visionary and most long-lasting contribution, however, was his development of St Saviour's as a focal point for the South London part of his diocese. He recognised that Rochester Cathedral could never be a spiritual centre for the clergy and people of South London, not least, which now seems extraordinary, because the clergy of South London could not afford the rail fare down to the Medway. He set in motion, and raised the money for, the rehabilitation of the church, and in particular for the demolition of the jerry-built nave and its replacement with a near-replica of its Mediaeval predecessor. The Diocese of Rochester had no suffragan bishop in those days, but Thorold appointed his friend William Barry, the recently retired Bishop of Sydney, as his Assistant Bishop with a special responsibility for South London and in particular for the development of St Saviour's. Barry retired in 1891, and his work was continued by Huyshe Yeatman-Biggs who was appointed the first Anglican Bishop of Southwark, not as a diocesan but as a suffragan of Rochester. Yeatman-Biggs described the people of his area as being "mostly poor, and as you approach the river from the south the poverty deepens to its darkest depth, and degradation runs it close until it finds St Saviour's, seated on her wretched throne, which forms the lowest depth".

Thorold wasn't able to oversee the completion of the rebuilding of the St Saviour's nave because, in 1892, he was appointed Bishop of Winchester. His successor at Rochester was Randall Davidson, and when Thorold died four years later Davidson succeeded him at Winchester, and later became Archbishop of Canterbury. The Bishop of Rochester who succeeded Davidson was Edward Stuart Talbot, sociable, urbane, a staunch Anglo-Catholic, and different from Thorold in almost every way. He made it clear from the outset that he saw South London as a higher priority than the Medway Towns, and he and his wife abandoned the traditional palace of the Bishops of Rochester in order to live at the newly acquired Bishop's House in Kennington. He expressed his intention to develop St Saviour's as a "white hot focus whence heat would flow into the surrounding district", and he was able to preside at its reopening in February 1897 with its new nave fully restored; the Prince of Wales was in attendance, together with the Duke and Duchess of Teck, the parents of his future daughter-in-law Queen Mary. He also revived as a Chapterhouse the Church of St Thomas's which had been abandoned since the move of St Thomas's Hospital to its present site opposite the Houses of Parliament, and the adjacent Queen Anne Treasurer's House as a residence for unmarried canons.

By 1900 there was general agreement in the places that mattered that South London should become a diocese in its own right, and the necessary measures were supported in principle by Lord Salisbury's Conservative Government. Five years elapsed, however, before Parliament got around to enacting the enabling legislation. Normal practice was that new dioceses, and there had recently been several, Liverpool in 1880, Newcastle in 1882, and Wakefield in 1888, were established by means of Private Member's Bills, but since it was widely expected that Talbot would become Southwark's first bishop, three such Bills were filibustered by a group of Evangelical Liberal MPs from the North of England. Salisbury was eventually prevailed upon to introduce a Government Bill, and the Diocese of Southwark came into being as a consequence of the necessary provisions being tacked onto the Bill which created the Diocese of Birmingham. It is interesting to note that not only did Talbot forego the ancient Diocese of Rochester in order to become Bishop of the new Diocese of Southwark, but that Bishop Gore of Worcester also chose to abandon his ancient see in order to become the first Bishop of Birmingham; appointed Bishop of Worcester in Gore's place was the former Suffragan Bishop of Southwark, Huyshe Yeatman-Biggs. Two new suffragan bishop posts were created at the same time as the Diocese of Southwark, Woolwich to which J.C.Leeke was appointed, and Kingston where the first incumbent was Cecil Hook. There was, however, an immediate problem in that there was no money to pay the suffragan bishops' salaries; the diocese was negatively endowed in the sense that Talbot had inherited debts but no capital, and he had to devote an inordinate amount of his episcopal time to fundraising, and to make savings which included decimating the cathedral's admired tradition of liturgical music developed by his predecessors. The celebrated organist and choir master Dr Madeley Richardson had to be sacked, and Talbot justified his action with the words "there is an opinion widely entertained that a service of such musical elaboration is more than a poor diocese can afford". Appointed in Richardson's place was a young organist called Edgar Cook, who later became a celebrated musician in his own right and remained in post for forty years till after the Second World War.

Whilst Bishop first of Rochester and then of Southwark, Talbot took a keen interest in education. He believed passionately in the benign impact on education not just of Christianity but of the Church of England in particular, and fought hard to preserve its denominational influence within the Board Schools; as a personal friend of Arthur Balfour he was able to influence the passage of the Education Act of 1902 (see page 55). He was also interested in the Church's overseas missionary work, making several visits to India and one to Africa, and playing an important role in the pivotal conference of the World Missionary Society held in Edinburgh in 1910. He moved on to become Bishop of Winchester in 1911, and died in 1934. Two Talbot Houses bear his name, the first a settlement in Camberwell, the women's equivalent of Cambridge House with which it is now amalgamated as "Cambridge House and Talbot", and the second in Poperinghe in Belgium, named after his son Neville who helped to found it as an army chaplain during World War I; it and its spin-offs became better known by their initials in First World War radio jargon, the equivalent of today's Tango Hotel, "Toc H".

During 1926 Garbett was able to move on to his second priority, which was the building of new churches. Despite the very rapid growth of South London's population (see page 14), he did not allow any money to be spent on new churches until he was satisfied that his existing clergy were being adequately paid. The growth in the population of his diocese was indeed astonishing; he said in 1927, "since the war, houses have been built for nearly 90,000 people, a population nearly as large as that of Bournemouth, and within a few years' time houses will have been built for 300,000, that is for a population larger than that of a great city like Newcastle-on-Tyne". His response was a "Twenty-five Churches Appeal" which aimed to raise £200,000. The appeal was launched by the Lord Mayor of London at the Mansion House with Archbishop Davidson as the principal speaker, and it was followed by a "Week of Prayer and Self-Denial" in November 1927 which culminated in a service at the cathedral where the collection alone amounted to £19,000. The success of this initiative had the perverse effect of causing everybody's enthusiasm to dry up even though the target hadn't quite been reached, but Garbett's determination drove him to make one final effort. He announced that, on Wednesday 27 June 1928, he would be sitting in the cathedral ready to receive donations, and such was his personal charisma that the donations came rolling in. He sat on his episcopal throne for fourteen hours without a break, in itself no mean physical feat, and all day long the donors filed in, starting with the vergers at 7 am and followed by a business man who had just commuted in to London Bridge and who donated a guinea on his own account together with 30/- which he had collected from the fellow travellers in his railway carriage. The people of the Rural Deanery of Newington marched in from the Elephant and Castle headed by a brass band, and groups of parishioners came from all over the diocese entering the cathedral singing their favourite hymns. He arranged for one hand-picked group to occupy one of the side-chapels to offer up intercessions, and for a second hand-picked group to occupy a neighbouring side-chapel to count up the money. The memorable day culminated at 9 pm with the singing of the *Te Deum*, and the bishop announcing to a packed cathedral that £7,840 had been handed in and that the target had thus been reached. The announcement was greeted by a long moment of silence more eloquent than applause, and it was broken by the ringing of the cathedral bells. Garbett later confessed that he had never before launched an appeal with such inward fear because he could not imagine how such an ambitious target could possibly be reached, but reached it was, and the twenty-five churches were duly built. The showpiece among them was St John's Catford, designed by Sir Charles Nicholson and built for £25,000. Garbett envisaged it as a second St Mary's Portsea, and he appointed to it Rev E.F.Edge-Partington MC, a former Portsea curate and a First World War hero with a dashing moustache, who served there with distinction for more than thirty years.

This success enabled Garbett to move on to his third priority, which was the enhancement of the cathedral. He was very aware that the diocese was still comparatively new and lacked a focal point, and he promoted the cathedral as being in a "working class area for a working class diocese"; most of the diocese is, in fact, suburban, but Garbett was not alone in perpetrating this denigration of his outer parishioners' suburban dream. Not all his initial efforts on behalf of the cathedral had been successful, however, and in 1923 he attended an interesting lunch at the Savoy Hotel which culminated in one of the diocese's most tantalising might-have-beens; John Reith, the Managing Director of the BBC, was keen to institute the practice, now commonplace, of broadcasting services live from churches, and had made a short list of two possible venues, Southwark Cathedral and St Martin-in-the-Fields. He invited Garbett and St Martin's flamboyant vicar Dick Sheppard to lunch with him so that the options could be discussed; both were enthusiastic, but in the event Reith decided in favour of St Martin's, perhaps because it was marginally handier for Bush House, and Southwark Cathedral had to wait almost half a century before it broadcast a service of its own. Garbett's underlying difficulty was that his cathedral was the poorest in the country, less well endowed even than several cathedrals which hadn't yet been built like Guildford, Portsmouth and Liverpool. The total amount available for the payment of cathedral clergy was £200 a year, which meant that Garbett had to combine the offices of Bishop and Dean, that Canon Haldane had to combine the office of Precentor with being vicar of a busy parish and Chaplain of Guy's, and that the canons had all to be honorary and spare-time. He later managed to secure a legacy which allowed for the appointment of a Sub-Dean to whom he delegated all his decanal responsibilities insofar as it was legally possible for him to do so, and later still, after the success of his Twenty-five Churches appeal, he was able to raise money for the payment of a Provost and some stipendiary canons. In 1930 he arranged the last of his show-piece cathedral events, a Procession of Witness in which seven thousand people marched to the cathedral from Kennington. He thoughtfully announced ahead of time that the culminating service would last no more than thirty-five minutes thus enabling parents to bring with them their small children, and that there would be no collection thus ensuring that the very poorest were not inhibited from attending.

Garbett's most lasting contribution to the Diocese of Southwark, however, was that he put it on the map. Prior to his episcopacy there had been a certain cachet in having served a title in the East End, but to have served in South London counted for very little. Garbett turned Southwark into a diocese where young ordinands wanted to come and work, and not just because of his success in raising clergy stipends. He was rigorous in his selection criteria and turned down more candidates than he accepted, and he was often frustrated by the way in which all that the candidates he had rejected had to do was cross the Thames in order to be accepted for ordination by A.F.Winnington-Ingram, the eccentric and lackadaisical Bishop of London. And Garbett also managed to make the challenge of serving in South London seem worthwhile. Back in the days when the area had been part of Winchester, it had been largely forgotten about because its problems had been deemed too difficult to solve; Thorold and Talbot had struggled with them, but it was Garbett who managed, at least to a degree, to demonstrate that it was possible for them to be successfully met. In 1932 he followed the well-rutted path, already trodden by Thorold, Davidson and Talbot, from South London to Winchester, and in 1942, in the middle of World War II, he was elevated to York, the only Southwark diocesan so far to have made it to Archbishop. He died on 31 December 1955.

Bishops Richard Parsons 1932-1942, and Bertram Simpson 1942-1959

Richard Godfrey Parsons was first and foremost an academic theologian. At Oxford he had contributed to "Foundations", the radical and controversial anthology which in some ways anticipated "Honest to God", and won himself a double first; bets were placed on whether it would be he or Temple who would ultimately make *Cantuar*. He was appointed Principal of Wells Theological College at the age of twenty-nine, and on the outbreak of the First World War moved to a parish in Manchester from where he was elevated to become the first Suffragan Bishop of Middleton. Geoffrey Fisher, one of his students at Wells, described him as "shy and diffident until you got to know him", so in terms of outward personality he was very different from Garbett, and he was also different from Garbett in that his health was never robust. Part of the thinking behind his appointment to Southwark had been that a theologian was needed to complement the worldliness of Bishop Winnington-Ingram on the other side of the river, but there were ways in which Parsons and the Diocese of Southwark were never really suited to one another. His early efforts at getting to know the diocese made him ill and he had to take a couple of months off, and he and his wife were unable to afford to keep open the whole of Bishop's House in Kennington and so had to live on the top floor which was converted into a rather unwelcoming flat. His aspirations were primarily to do with building; he wanted to build more church schools, and more new churches for the still expanding suburbs, and housing for poor people on a site which had become available between Waterloo Bridge and County Hall. He lacked the charisma as a fund-raiser of either Talbot or Garbett, however, and didn't get very far, and his riverside site remained unbuilt on till 1951 when it was used for the Festival of Britain; it is now home to the Festival Hall, the Royal National Theatre and the London Eye. To be fair to him, the early part of his episcopacy was dominated first by economic recession and then by the anxiety provoked by the rise to power first of Mussolini and then of Hitler, but he does not seem to have shown any particular interest in either of these phenomena as issues which needed addressing in their own right. One personal triumph was his revision in 1937 of the statutes governing the cathedral's constitution. The care of the building was entrusted to a Provost who was also Rector of the parish, and an Administrative Chapter was established comprising six residential canons, together with a General Chapter which also included the suffragan bishops, the archdeacons, and a sprinkling of laity.

There are still a few clergy around, inevitably now very old, who remember Bishop Parsons. They talk of him as gentle, always polite, and always willing to listen, but also as well guarded and hesitant in his responses to what he was told. These clergy also describe what it was like being an incumbent during the 1930s; life was more tranquil than it became later, and the emphasis was very much on visiting parishioners in their own homes, and on preparing elaborate visiting schedules to impress the archdeacon which ensured that nobody was being missed and that every christening, confirmation and marriage was being annually followed up. As clergy they were always deferred to, at least in part because they were graduates at a time when very few other people were, and there were many fewer meetings because the assumption was that the vicar knew best and therefore had no need for help or advice. Anglo-Catholic churches had their Parish Mass as the main Sunday service, but in most churches the focal point was Matins, with Communion celebrated early in the morning and Evensong in the late afternoon. There was a strong convention that clergy should fast until the Eucharist had been celebrated, and Anglo-Catholic vicars in particular talk about the difficulty of surviving to the end of an 11.00 Mass on an empty stomach.

But then came the Second World War. As well as being Bishop of Southwark Parsons was also the official visitor to the White Russian community in Paris, and he found himself marooned in Paris when war was declared. He managed to get himself back to London without very much difficulty, but he had to leave behind him all his episcopal vestments. During the first month of the Blitz in 1940 twenty churches in his diocese were destroyed, and seventy more were damaged; he felt the pain of this personally and found it difficult to respond, and in February 1941 he was again ordered by his doctors to take time off because of illness. His episcopal responsibilities were devolved to Fred Hawkes, the urbane and imperturbable Bishop of Kingston, who reported that, by May 1941, one hundred and fifty churches had been hit, but added "We have been delivered from a large number of hideous stained glass windows, for which we cannot be too thankful". The windows of the cathedral were also shattered, and the organist Edgar Cook, bravely planning a performance of Bach's St Matthew Passion, regretfully announced its cancellation "owing to enemy action". From then on a team of fire-watchers

Bishop Bertram Simpson opening the rebuilt St Anne's Kennington, 1951

camped out in the cathedral most nights armed with buckets of water so that they could mitigate the effects of incendiary bombs; most of the team were office workers from the City who had to be back at their desks the following morning.

Parsons returned to his diocese for a brief period, but in 1942 moved on to become Bishop of Hereford from where, in 1946, he was able to return to Paris and retrieve his vestments which had miraculously survived intact throughout the war. His successor, Bertram Simpson, is the only Bishop of Southwark so far to have been born and brought up within the diocese. He came from Selhurst and enjoyed and understood the suburbs, and he also enjoyed and understood being a parish priest. Despite being a South Londoner he was ordained at St Paul's, and he became first an outstanding vicar of the fashionable church of St Peter's Cranleigh Gardens, and later suffragan Bishop of Kensington. After his appointment to Southwark had been announced, but prior to taking it up, he crossed the river *incognito* to have a look at his new cathedral, and he recorded in his diary that it was a miserable November afternoon, and that the cathedral was empty and its windows all boarded up, but that the welcome he received from one of the vergers inspired him to make the best of the circumstances in which he was going to find himself. He made a point at his enthronement in February 1942 of inviting to the service all the churches in exile, Dutch, Danish and Norwegian, and also the Greek and Russian Orthodox Bishops. People's spiritual awareness became greatly heightened during and after the war, and Simpson recognised the importance of encouraging it and giving it scope for expression. He embarked upon a mission to air raid shelters, seeing this as an opportunity for "getting alongside all sorts and conditions of men", and inside the shelters he held *impromptu* ecumenical services which invariably ended with a singing of "Abide with Me". He also supported and encouraged others in this sort of work, especially Cuthbert Bardsley and Colin Cuttell in Woolwich (see page 37). He also made the cathedral available to a variety of gatherings at which a whole gamut of topics were discussed, and this practice was developed both by Bardsley when he became Provost in 1944, and also by his successor Hugh Ashdown. Simpson also attached a high priority to supporting the clergy of the parishes which had suffered the worst of the bomb damage, especially those where the churches had been destroyed and where services were having to happen in borrowed premises. Quite a few parishes had to do without clergy altogether, because of attrition and the demand for manpower elsewhere, and several of them had to be looked after by women, and Simpson gave them every help and encouragement. One casualty of the bombing was Bishop's House which was totally destroyed, and he had to move to a small house in Wimbledon and commute from there to the diocesan office which squatted in temporary premises near the Oval.

The coming of peace did not mean an immediate return to how things had been before the war. South London's social dislocation was too severe for any quick fix, and people's main concerns were with restoring their homes, rebuilding their families in the aftermath of military service and the evacuation of the children, and trying to make the best of rationing and the disruptions to services. Simpson recognised these secular priorities, and set the Church to help. The role of the parochial clergy in maintaining the secular bureaucracy during and after the war is often forgotten; incumbents were constantly having to certify that people were who they said they were, to hold pensions for them and payments for wives whose husbands were absent overseas, to oversee evacuation procedures and later the children's return, and to serve on local committees as the Welfare State was getting itself laboriously established. And then, after presiding over most the 1940s, Simpson also presided over almost all the 1950s. The transition, and it was a big one, was marked by the Festival of Britain and by the election of a Conservative Government. Life started getting back to what most people thought of as normal, and normal included re-establishing the habit of churchgoing. St John's Waterloo was designated as the Festival of Britain Church and offered visitors the opportunity for quiet reflection and prayer, and a great many people took the offer up, and the cathedral also contributed by staging a modern morality play. In 1953 the Archbishop of Canterbury called for all churches to be open so that prayers could be said for the coronation of Queen Elizabeth II, and in 1955 the new Queen came with her husband to Southwark Cathedral to help celebrate the diocese's Golden Jubilee. Simpson continued his work of quiet but effective consolidation till he retired in 1959, and he died in 1972.

Bishop Mervyn Stockwood 1959-1980, South Bank Religion

Mervyn Stockwood was enthroned as Bishop of Southwark in May 1959. Prior to this he had spent nineteen years in the parish of St Matthew Moorfields in Bristol, and then four as Vicar of Great St Mary's, the University Church in Cambridge. Soon after his appointment had been announced he preached a sermon at Great St Mary's in which he asked the question, "How can the Church come alongside the people?", and he illustrated the difficulty by imagining himself, as bishop, talking to a working man on a wharf on the Thames and having no language in which to get the Christian message across. It is difficult for people nowadays to imagine just how conservative the Church of England of the 1950s actually was; the standard texts were the Book of Common Prayer and the King James's Bible, the thirty-nine articles were insisted upon as the Anglican norm, ordination training happened only in small residential colleges and only for men, the most commonly attended service was Matins, and in a large majority of churches Holy Communion was celebrated only at inconvenient hours, without music, and by a priest standing with his back to his congregation. There were stirrings for change, but none of them commanded any degree of widespread support, and few during Simpson's episcopacy had trickled down to the south of the Thames.

In his Enthronement Sermon, Stockwood stressed the need for vision; "Where there is no vision", he said, misquoting the Book of Proverbs, "the people perish". The question he asked was, "How can we express the faith in words that are meaningful to a contemporary generation, and take into consideration other branches of knowledge and categories of thought? We should not be afraid to admit that, while we accept without compromise the basic concepts of the Christian revelation, there are many things about which we are ignorant and must reserve our judgement, many things in human experience that seem to contradict our claims, and come what may we will follow where truth leads and always be intellectually honest and spiritually humble". Whilst affirming the parochial system, he called for it to be supplemented by "cautious experiments in a new type of priesthood and a new type of organisation; it is possible that a man who works in industry and is also ordained will be better able to understand the needs and outlook of his associates than one who, because of his status as a parochial clergyman, is inevitably to some extent segregated". In this sermon, Stockwood set himself three immediate challenges: the revitalising of parochial ministry particularly in the poor areas along the riverbank, the creation of a supplementary priesthood, and the development of a new and more relevant liturgy.

Central to his strategy for addressing the first of these Enthronement Sermon challenges was the appointment to a number of riverbank parishes clergy teams comprising as many as ten priests, three or so of them full time pastors in the conventional sense, and the remainder earning their living in the secular world. Teams like this were established in Woolwich under Nick Stacey, in Deptford under David Diamond, in Bermondsey under Bill Skelton, and in Eltham under Barney Milligan. The Woolwich team became the best known, not least because of Stacey's gift for publicity, and it developed in St Mary's Church a creche for babies, a lunchtime cafe, a discotheque in the crypt, and offices in the galleries for the Citizens' Advice Bureau, the Greenwich Council for Social Service, the Samaritans, and the Quadrant Housing Association which Stacey had helped to start. But then, in December 1964, Stacey wrote an article for the Observer entitled "Failure of a Mission". He said that, for nearly five years, he had led one of the largest and ablest teams of clergy anywhere in England, and had "played every card in the pack", and had initiated everything he had set out to, but had achieved nothing; "We have failed", he cataclysmically said. But the Woolwich team did, in fact, achieve a great deal. Quadrant became one of the largest and most successful housing associations in London, specialising in rehabilitating small houses in poor areas. A Family Planning Association clinic was set up, and a reception centre for homeless people in Plumstead, both of which lasted. Interdenominational working was pioneered with a Methodist minister, Ray Billington, appointed as a full member of the team, preaching and taking services, and St Mary's was shared with a Presbyterian congregation thus provoking the Sharing of Churches Act which was passed by Parliament in 1969. The other teams were similarly innovative, the Bermondsey team pioneering industrial mission and assisting Richard Carr-Gomm in developing shared housing schemes for poor and lonely people through the Morpeth and Abbeyfield Societies, and the Eltham team doing innovative work in race relations and forging links with the Diocese of the Windward Islands. The sole criterion against which Stacey measured his declared failure was that of increasing the size of his congregation. Stockwood, defending the Observer article, asked the question, "Why is it that men appear to respond more readily in Reigate, Purley and Coulsdon than in Walworth, Woolwich and Battersea?", but on that occasion he offered no answer. Stacey left Church employment in 1965 to become Deputy Director of Oxfam, and later Director of Social Services for Kent.

Only one month after his Enthronement Sermon, at his first Diocesan Conference in June 1959, Stockwood outlined his plans for addressing the second of the challenges he had set himself. He announced that he intended introducing a new method of ordination training for "graduates who will earn their living by day and at night will go ahead with their theological studies; when they reach ordination level they may become curates in the ordinary way, or they may feel they can be of greater use if they remain where they are and discover their way to a new pattern of priesthood." He was fortunate in that, shortly before his enthronement, the post of Bishop of Woolwich had fallen vacant and, even prior to taking up his appointment, he had written to Archbishop Geoffrey Fisher complaining that the central team he was about to inherit, the Bishop of Kingston, the Provost of the Cathedral and the three archdeacons, were "all essentially conventional churchmen; I use the word `conventional' in no unkindly sense, but to describe an attitude". The man he wanted as Bishop of Woolwich, he said in his letter, "must be a man who (1) understands what I am trying to do, (2) has the intellectual competence and theological knowledge to advise me, (3) is accustomed to dealing with and training ordinands, and (4), while having a special concern for experimental work, can at the same time do the normal pastoral and routine duties of a suffragan Bishop". What he was in effect doing was writing a job description tailor-made to fit his Cambridge friend John Robinson, the Dean of Clare College, who had earlier been his curate in Bristol and later a lecturer at the Theological College at Wells. Although concerns were raised in a number of high places about the wisdom of the choice, Stockwood appointed Robinson as Bishop of Woolwich before the year was out.

Robinson was charged with the implementation of Stockwood's vision of a supplementary priesthood, and he did so with quite remarkable speed. He drew up a schema for the Southwark Ordination Course (SOC) which was approved by Stockwood in January 1960, and which was provisionally approved by the Central Advisory Council for the Ministry (CACTM) in March. SOC then started with thirty-one ordinands in September of the same year. Initial thinking was that the SOC training sessions should take place in the cathedral, but Robinson didn't like the idea of it happening "over the shop". He arranged for the academic teaching to take place at Christchurch Blackfriars, already home to SLIM, but he also felt strongly the need for a rural retreat where the students could live together as a community, even if only for weekends. The obvious place to start looking was the Surrey countryside, and this would carry with it the additional advantage of strengthening the cathedral's links with the southern part of the diocese. Uvedale Lambert was a wealthy high churchman who owned a large estate near Godstone on which the second best house, Wychcroft, was surplus to his requirements. He had previously lent it to the Community of the Resurrection in Mirfield for conferences, and to Catholic Mission for short training courses, and Robinson negotiated that it should be made available to SOC. SOC didn't need it all the time, so Douglas Rhymes, formerly the Vicar of New Eltham who became Canon Librarian of the Cathedral in 1962 which also required him to act as Diocesan Lay Training Officer, was brought in to help fill its spare capacity. Wychcroft has played an important part in the life of the diocese ever since.

Only seven of SOC's initial thirty-one ordinands were graduates, eighteen had been to secondary school, and six had been only to Elementary School. The course's first Principal was Stanley Evans, but he was tragically killed in a car crash in 1965 and was succeeded by his deputy Frank Colquhoun. Other lecturers during the Stockwood era included Cecilia Goodenough, Benedicta Whistler, Peter Selby the future Bishop of Kingston, and Gerald Hudson who succeeded Colquhoun as Principal in 1971. SOC was given full CACTM recognition in 1965 which allowed it to start enrolling ordinands from other dioceses, and in 1967 it recruited the first woman to train for the ministry alongside men, Una Kroll. In 1974 it became ecumenical, enrolling its first

Methodist ordinand who was soon followed by ordinands from the United Reformed and Lutheran Churches, and by interested Roman Catholics. About half the ordinands trained on SOC were ordained to the non-stipendiary ministry, and most of these defined themselves as Ministers in Secular Employment (MSEs), seeing their ministry as focused on their places of work (see page 39). In 1994 SOC amalgamated with similar courses based in Canterbury and Chichester to become the South Eastern Institute for Theological Education (SEITE), and the new institute relocated to Chatham whilst retaining Wychcroft as one of its residential bases.

The key player in addressing the third of Stockwood's Enthronement Sermon challenges was Ernest Southcott, formerly the Vicar of Halton in Leeds. In 1961 George Reindorp, the Provost of the Cathedral whom Stockwood had inherited, moved on to become Bishop of Guildford, and Southcott was appointed his successor. He quickly introduced a number of liturgical innovations at the cathedral which were seen as radical at the time but which are now taken for granted; for Sunday morning Eucharists the altar was moved forward to the top of the nave and the priest who was celebrating stood behind it facing the congregation, the Bible readings were read by laymen and laywomen, and the Peace was shared throughout the congregation. He also introduced a range of special interest services, including for the disabled and for the mentally ill, and he used the cathedral as a forum for public debate, arranging a series of Garbett Lectures with a gamut of distinguished speakers some of whom were known to be atheists, and a number of dialogues with the directors of Voluntary Organisations such as Alcoholics Anonymous and the National Society for Mentally Handicapped Children. At the same time Stockwood deliberately encouraged a range of liturgical experiments which were tried out in various contexts within the diocese; Stacey in Woolwich introduced a new liturgy for baptism, and Stockwood himself presided at a series of services for Holy Week devised at St Peter's Streatham. Douglas Rhymes introduced new forms both of private and of corporate prayer, as well as delivering several series of somewhat radical lectures on ethics. At the same time, other art forms were also pioneered within the diocese. Geoffrey Beaumont, the Vicar of St George's Camberwell, had written his Folk Mass in 1956, and this was followed by a myriad of experiments in church music, some using rock groups and electric guitars. Sidney Carter was asked to write new hymns for some of the Cathedral's special occasions, and at least two of them have now become a regular part of every church's repertoire, "One more step along the world I go" which was written for a school leavers' service, and "When I needed a neighbour were you there" which he wrote for Christian Aid Week. The artist John Hayward made several contributions, his best known being the portrait of Christ the Worker which hangs in the chapel at Wychcroft. In 1960 Stockwood commended a book by Peter Hammond entitled "Liturgy and Architecture" which advocated a new design for church buildings using either a circle or semi-circle with the altar at its focal point; the first new church to be built in the diocese during Stockwood's episcopacy, St Mary's Peckham, put these principles into practice, designed by Robert Potter and Richard Hare and consecrated in 1962.

One immediate problem which confronted Stockwood on his arrival in Southwark was that he had nowhere to live. Bishop's House in Kennington had been destroyed by bombing during the war, and his predecessor had lived in his own small house in Wimbledon. Stockwood found temporary accommodation in a flat north of the river, and engaged one of his many aristocratic women friends, Lady Elizabeth Cavendish, to house-hunt for him. Lady Elizabeth soon discovered an Edwardian mansion in Tooting Bec Gardens which she deemed suitable for the unusual combination of worship, office-work and entertainment, and the bishop and his mother moved in.

During his early years Stockwood found himself on a number of occasions having to enforce ecclesiastical discipline, and this was inevitably difficult for a bishop who saw himself as radical and liberal. One, which happened only a few months into his episcopacy, involved an elderly curate in Carshalton who insisted on using the Roman Rite when celebrating Communion; Stockwood ended up locking him out of the church where he had been licensed to officiate, and the case was widely reported in the press. A second was the case of Bryn Thomas, vicar of the Church of the Ascension Balham Hill, who was accused in 1960 by one of his female parishioners of sexual impropriety; his case was tried in the Consistory Court where the Diocesan Chancellor Garth Moore found him guilty, and Thomas was publicly unfrocked in May 1961. Stockwood later admitted that he had handled both these cases very badly, generating unfortunate national publicity, causing Thomas in particular unnecessary humiliation, and creating a breach between Stockwood and Moore which was never properly healed. Another less unfortunate disciplinary issue concerned Canon John Pearce-Higgins, the Vice-Provost of the Cathedral, who voiced his difficulty in accepting the Thirty-Nine Articles as the standard of doctrinal orthodoxy; he said that he saw the Articles as a Reformation document which had been topical and relevant at the time but which had long since outlived its usefulness. Stockwood supported Pearce-Higgins, a stand which was bitterly opposed by Evangelical clergy within the diocese, but the episode led to the setting up of a Doctrine Commission and in due course to a greatly modified form of assent.

The phrase "South Bank Religion" was first coined by Stockwood in an article for the Evening Standard on 11 July 1963, and the two icons of South Bank Religion were Stockwood himself and John Robinson, whose time as Bishop of Woolwich coincided with the first decade of Stockwood's episcopacy. Within months of his arrival in the diocese, Robinson attracted national notoriety by agreeing to appear as an expert witness at the trial for obscenity of Penguin Books which followed the publication of the unexpurgated version of "Lady Chatterley's Lover". Robinson described Lawrence as "always trying to portray sex as something sacred, in a real sense as an act of holy communion". He specifically stressed his use of lower case letters for holy communion, and conceded that "the kind of sexual relationship depicted in the book is not one which I would necessarily regard as ideal", but he was nevertheless immediately and severely censured by Archbishop Fisher, though Stockwood stood by him. The Archbishop's disapproval, however, cut little public ice; Penguin Books were acquitted, and the general acclaim which greeted the verdict indicated that public opinion was ready for the change. Robinson was undoubtedly courageous in taking the stand that he did, but perhaps also somewhat naive in that the effect of his defence of Lawrence's neo-paganism was to link him indissolubly in the minds of many with moral relativism and the permissive society, and it was these associations which came to define the public perception of South Bank Religion.

And then, in 1963, Robinson published "Honest to God". Never has a small paperback made so great an impact, and never has such an impact been so unexpected, and never has the impact generated by a such small book had so little to do with the book's actual content. Robinson later said that, like so many things in the Church of England, "Honest to God" had started with a minor accident. He had been bending over one day to tie his shoelace and had cricked his back, and this meant that he had had to spend several weeks in bed and, while he was in his bed, he found himself thinking, as might have been expected of a bishop, about God. He decided that he would commit his thoughts to paper, and "Honest to God" was the result. Reading the book today makes one wonder what all the fuss was about, but fuss there certainly was, and the fuss was totally disproportionate to the book itself. The book ran through eight editions in the first three months, and people who wanted to read it had to queue up for copies if they were lucky or wait for the next edition to come out if they weren't. Its publication provoked heated arguments about Christianity in pubs and coffee bars throughout the country, and in large measure the controversy was the consequence of an article by Ivan Yates which appeared in The Observer the Sunday before the book was published which proclaimed, in banner headlines, "OUR IMAGE OF GOD MUST GO", and which defined the terms in which the book was read. By and large the book was enthusiastically received by people who had been brought up as churchgoers but had stopped going because they were finding it irrelevant or boring, and it deeply upset a great many committed churchgoers who felt betrayed by being told, by no less a person than a consecrated

The Best Seller of 1963

bishop, that their faith was out of date and all wrong anyway. An enormous amount of correspondence was generated, and this was later brought together in a follow-up book entitled "The Need for Certainty" edited by Robert Towler, and David Edwards published a more digestible volume called "The Honest to God Debate" which included a selection of letters, essays and reviews. The people to whom "Honest to God" seemed to mean most were members of the caring professions like teachers, doctors, nurses, social workers and psychotherapists, whose numbers were then increasing rapidly, who were not churchgoers but still wanted to call themselves Christians, and who were looking for an authentication for the altruistic work to which they were committed.

The starting point of "Honest to God" was Robinson's view, which he shared with Stockwood, that the way in which God was being presented and talked about was no longer relevant to contemporary society. His intention in addressing this issue was essentially missionary, in that the task he set himself was that of providing people with a new way of looking at God, and with a new language which they could use when doing so. The old fashioned thinking which Robinson felt needed to be abandoned and moved on from was the anthropomorphised view of God as a "Father", and the situationalised location of God as being "up there". The language used in the Bible is all about God being situated somewhere up above the world we live in and, from this superior vantage point, looking down on us mere mortals and observing what we are doing and taking an overview of everything that's going on. Occasionally God comes "down" to earth, but if we really want to encounter him we have to go "up" to heaven. In Robinson's view this way of looking at things had both theological and spiritual implications, since it encouraged people to think of God as being outside them rather than inside them, and judging them, albeit with a fatherly concern. Another aspect of traditional thinking which Robinson addressed was to do with morality. In "Honest to God" he expressed the view that it was no longer viable for the Church to preach a prescriptive morality which told people what was right and what was wrong; he saw this as being much too simplistic and proposed instead that our predicaments should be viewed in the light of God's love for us and our love for God. And he also addressed the issue of the incarnation. Instead of seeing Jesus as God having descended to earth, he suggested that we should see Jesus as a human being who was so in touch with God that he could be described as being God, and that because of his Godliness he was both a model and an exemplar for us human beings, a "man for others".

In "Honest to God" Robinson drew heavily on three German Protestant theologians, Martin Buber, Paul Tillich and Dietrich Bonhoeffer. His main borrowing from Buber was the phrase "I/Thou". Buber said that there were two different ways of relating to things outside ourselves; either we can observe them scientifically and dispassionately while holding ourselves aloof, for which he coined the phrase "I/It", or we can relate to them subjectively and personally which he describes as "I/Thou" (*Ich/Du* in German). He saw our relationship with God as being "I/Thou" since it is essentially a personal relationship which we cannot stand aloof from. The phrase which Robinson borrowed from Tillich was "ground of our being", which Tillich uses as a means of describing the way that we become aware of God's meaning for us; we know we exist, we know that we are motivated by things that are important to us and which transcend our everyday concerns, and this is the "ground of our being". And the phrase he borrowed from Bonhoeffer, less accurately and more controversially, was "religionless Christianity", which he took as implying that it was possible to relate to God without going to church.

The publication of "Honest to God" meant that Robinson became very much in demand as a public speaker, and he managed to fit in several extensive foreign lecture tours, especially in the United States, alongside his demanding schedule as Bishop of Woolwich. Very often his attempts to amplify the ideas expressed in "Honest to God" proved as controversial as the book itself. He continued to write prolifically, and merely listing the titles of the other books which he published give an indication of the line he was taking: "On Being the Church in the World" (1961), "The New Reformation?" (1965), "Exploration into God" (1965), "But that I can't believe!" (1967), and "Christian Freedom in a Permissive Society" (1970). In 1969 he retired from Woolwich to become Dean of Chapel at Trinity College, Cambridge, and he died of cancer in 1983.

Bishop Mervyn Stockwood 1959-1980, The Second Decade

Less may seem to have happened during the second decade of Stockwood's episcopacy than during the first, but throughout the seventies the innovations which had been so loudly trumpeted in the sixties were being more quietly consolidated and implemented. Stockwood and his suffragans continued to attach a high priority to the pastoral care of their clergy, and a practice was instituted of summoning all the clergy of the diocese for residential jamborees at Butlin's Holiday Camps every four years. But Stockwood never lost sight of the three challenges he had set himself in his Enthronement Sermon, and by any criteria the second and third of them were successfully met. The Southwark Ordination Course continued to flourish and rapidly became accepted as a new model for ordination training, and was widely copied elsewhere. Alongside it the concept and practice of Ministry in Secular Employment was developed and pioneered, and it too was also widely copied outside the diocese. And at the same time the liturgies pioneered by Southcott and others continued to develop, contributing to and borrowing from Series II and Series III which in turn became accepted as orthodoxy and formed the basis of the ASB, the Alternative Services Book, which was published in 1980. Peter Penwarden, Vice-Provost from 1971 till 1991, continued to develop liturgies for special occasions and to supplement them by the creative use of music.

The first of the Enthronement Sermon challenges, the rejuvenation of the poorer parishes along the riverbank, inevitably proved more intractable. In 1969 Robinson was succeeded as Bishop of Woolwich by a no less celebrated figure, the Evangelical cricketer David Sheppard, who had previously been Warden and Chaplain of the Mayflower Centre in Canning Town. Sheppard's celebrity rested in part on his achievements as an England batsman, which included touring Australia in 1962-63 when a clergyman of seven years standing, and in part on the role he played in the 1968 D'Oliviera controversy when he took on the MCC for failing to select a black cricketer from Worcestershire to tour South Africa; in the event D'Oliviera was added to the nominated team, causing South Africa's President Vorster to cancel the tour. Sheppard was later to publish a book entitled "Bias to the Poor", and an early indication of this bias was his refusal to live in the Robinsons' house in Blackheath; he and his family moved instead to Asylum Road in Peckham, a street in which even then the majority of the residents were black. He committed himself to bringing black people more closely into the parochial and diocesan mainstream; he chaired the Martin Luther King Foundation, and brought into his area, as Vicar of St Lawrence Catford, the Barbadian Wilfred Wood who had been ordained in the Diocese of London and was later to become the first Bishop of Croydon. Another future bishop he persuaded into South East London was Jim Thompson, who became Team Rector of Thamesmead before moving on to become Bishop first of Stepney and then of Bath and Wells. Sheppard, like Robinson and Stockwood himself, was a conscientious pastor to his clergy, and one of his contributions was the creation of the post of Borough Dean; he persuaded Stockwood to commission a study by the Industrial Society on how the diocese was run, and the outcome was the introduction of a system of "structured reviews" of each incumbent's objectives and achievements, and the appointment of a Borough Dean to an area coterminous with each London Borough as a means of strengthening the diocese's middle management. In 1975 he was appointed Bishop of Liverpool, and ironically it was from there that he was to make his greatest contribution to the rejuvenation of the poorer parishes along the riverbank, as a leading member of the Archbishops' Commission on Urban Priority Areas whose report was published in 1985 as "Faith in the City". He was succeeded as Bishop of Woolwich by Michael Marshall.

In 1970 William Gilpin announced his intention to retire as Bishop of Kingston; Stockwood had inherited him and had consistently failed to appreciate his steady integrity, and the two of them had never seen eye to eye. As Gilpin's replacement Stockwood chose Hugh Montefiore, his successor-but-one as Vicar of Great St Mary's in Cambridge and another strong personality whose successes and failures were both on a grand scale. One of the components of South Bank Religion, and the one which attracted the most media interest, was the frank discussion of sexual ethics; Robinson had contributed, his pronouncements attracting maximum attention because of Lady Chatterley, and so had Douglas Rhymes. And Montefiore had made his own contribution from Cambridge, going public on the idea that Jesus might possibly have been homosexual. It was generally assumed that as a consequence of this indiscretion he would never make it to a mitre, but a series of intrigues involving Stockwood, Rab Butler as Master of Trinity College Cambridge, and Eric James, Trinity's former chaplain and later Vicar of St George's Camberwell, resulted in his appointment to Kingston. In 1977 he was appointed Bishop of Birmingham, and was succeeded at Kingston by Keith Sutton, who later became Bishop of Lichfield.

Stockwood had earlier announced his intention of retiring on the twentieth anniversary of his consecration, but in the event he decided to stay on to preside over the celebration of the diocese's seventy-fifth jubilee. On 13 July 1980 there was an open air Eucharist on the Centre Court at Wimbledon attended by eleven thousand people, most of whom had brought picnics. Communion was distributed by over one hundred clergy, and the celebration also included a Parsons versus People rugby match, a fun run, a hymn writing competition, and specially manufactured T-shirts. Stockwood then retired on 30 September 1980 after just over twenty-one years in office. He died in Bath on 13 January 1995.

Without doubt Mervyn Stockwood was one of the most charismatic and flamboyant churchmen of the twentieth century and, though his period in office coincided with a catastrophic decline in church attendance, he probably did more than any other single person to hold the decline in check. The general consensus is that he was deeply conscientious in his own spiritual discipline, and that in the pastoral care of his clergy he was unrivalled, earning even from those of them with whom he crossed swords a deep respect, gratitude and love. He attracted outstanding men into his diocese to work with him; three of the five suffragans he appointed went on to be diocesan bishops, David Sheppard to Liverpool, Hugh Montefiore to Birmingham, and Keith Sutton to Lichfield, and his appointees to the staff of the cathedral were equally illustrious. And yet there always seemed to be question marks about him, in large measure because of the ambiguities and tensions at the heart of his personality and attitudes. He was charismatic, gregarious and extrovert and craved publicity, but at the same time he was lonely and insecure, in part no doubt because of his homosexuality of which he made little secret. He professed an ideological socialism, but was at the same time a *bon viveur* who enjoyed the high life, hobnobbing with royalty and the aristocracy. He made several visits east of the Iron Curtain, in particular to Russia and to Romania, and often came back to make unfortunate remarks, both in the press and in the House of Lords, about the desirability of life under Communism, but at the same time he was especially friendly with Princess Margaret, the only person on record to have told him to shut up because he was being a bore, and with Prince Charles, who confided in him during many of the crises in his life; an indication of Stockwood's loyalty to the Prince is that, shortly before his death, he ordered all their correspondence to be destroyed and none of it has survived. Another unlikely friendship was with Dame Barbara Cartland, a fellow *prima donna*, and he was a frequent visitor to Althorp where, prior to her marriage, Lady Diana Spencer used to bring him breakfast in bed. He declared his egalitarianism, professing his identification with South London's poor and unchurched and using his position as a Member of the House of Lords to advocate a number of left-wing causes on which the Church had rarely spoken out, but there was no one more conscious of hierarchy or of his own position at the top of it, and the discipline he imposed was authoritarian. He was a great showman whilst pretending not to be; he announced on his arrival in the diocese that he would never wear episcopal gaiters, but he always wore instead a flowing purple cassock which created an even greater theatrical effect. Nick Stacey once suggested in public that he wear purple pyjamas in place of mass vestments, and as a consequence he was jokingly presented with scores of pairs of purple pyjamas donated to him from all over the world. Throughout his episcopacy neither he nor his diocese were ever out of the news for very long, and he was described both as a "Pillar of the Establishment" and also as a "Column of the Evening Standard", but at the same time he never properly mastered the art of "spin" and the publicity he deliberately provoked was more often hostile than not, though he frequently defended his actions as a modern method of getting the Church's message across. He hoped for preferment but no offer ever came, and he was deeply disappointed in 1974 when he was not invited to succeed either Michael Ramsay as Archbishop of Canterbury or Donald Coggan as Archbishop of York; his aspiration was perhaps naive, particularly since he consistently despised and avoided General Synod, and rumour has it that he was never considered to be a "safe enough pair of hands". And there are question marks too about what he actually achieved. He promised so much, and staked a disproportionate claim over whatever he initiated that was novel and new, and as a consequence he was disproportionately blamed for all that he failed to deliver. But he was certainly memorable, and the memories of those who knew him are always underpinned by affection because the hurts that he caused by his frequent outbursts of bad behaviour were always offset by even more frequent instances of charm, care and compassion.

Bishops Ronald Bowlby 1980-1991, Roy Williamson 1991-98, and Tom Butler, 1998-

The most significant characteristic of Ronnie Bowlby, who was appointed Bishop of Southwark in 1980, was that he wasn't Mervyn Stockwood. By the end of Stockwood's long episcopacy the diocese was in a state of exhaustion; for two decades it had been under perpetual media scrutiny, everyone everywhere had been under pressure always to do something special or to come up with something new, and Stockwood's maverick personality and unpredictable behaviour had generated their own tensions and anxieties. Bowlby's arrival signalled quieter times, and an opportunity to relax and get back properly to work. The differences between him and his predecessor were pronounced. He was an Old Etonian and was able to wear his upper class provenance with humility and, unlike Stockwood, he felt no need for public display. He believed in delegation, and reorganised the diocesan Areas into almost free-standing units under the leadership of their suffragans. And, most tellingly, whereas Stockwood had personally dominated his senior staff meetings and had used them for the most part for rubber stamping decisions he had already made elsewhere, Bowlby introduced a system of rotating chairmanship and relegated himself to *primus inter pares*. He came to Southwark from being Bishop of Newcastle, and his two successors were also already diocesans, perhaps an indication that the diocese had come to be seen as a senior appointment, or perhaps a belated recognition on the part of the powers-that-be that it was handy to have at Southwark a bishop who was already a member of the House of Lords.

As well as being already a member of the House of Lords, Bowlby was also already a member of a group of bishops whom Archbishop Robert Runcie had called together to advise him on urban affairs. This was a consequence of an initiative triggered by Eric James, the former vicar of St George's Camberwell, who rightly anticipated that the plight of the country's inner cities was about to get worse rather than better under the newly elected Government of Margaret Thatcher, given her well publicised commitment to freeing up individual enterprise, which in most inner city areas was in short supply, at the expense of any transfer of resources from rich to poor. Runcie's group also included three Southwark "old boys", David Sheppard, Hugh Montefiore, and Jim Thompson who by then had become Bishop of Stepney. It duly recommended the setting up of an Archbishops' Commission on Urban Priority Areas, which was soon convened under the chairmanship of Sir Richard O'Brien, formerly of the Manpower Service's Commission. After two years' work, in December 1985, it published its report under the title "Faith in the City". The report made recommendations to Government, to the Church, and to urban parishes themselves. As might have been expected, the recommendations to Government were highly critical of Margaret Thatcher's policies, and as a consequence, even before the report was published, the Government put effort into denigrating it, branding it as Marxist and taking the line that the Church should confine its attention to religion and leave politics to elected politicians. In large measure this assault backfired, increasing both the amount of publicity which the report generated and also the degree of public sympathy which it inspired.

"Faith in the City" may or may not have had some influence on the policies of the Thatcher Government, but it undoubtedly had a major impact on policy making within the Church. In accordance with the report's recommendations, Urban Priority Areas, or UPAs, were identified and given a higher profile and a more generous allocation of resources, the Church Urban Fund, from which Southwark disproportionately benefited, was set up to finance special projects, and a new office was established in Lambeth Palace to monitor the spending of the money and progress on the recommendations' implementation. Within the diocese responsibility for implementing "Faith in the City" was given to Peter Hall, whom Bowlby had appointed Bishop of Woolwich in succession to Michael Marshall, and Hall worked hard both to divert resources and skilled manpower into the poorer parishes along the riverbank, and also to ensure that the parishes themselves defined their objectives and quantified the resources available to them in order to increase the likelihood that their objectives would be met. One parish that performed particularly well was Christchurch Brixton, then still suffering the after-effects of the 1981 Brixton riots, where the setting up of small local businesses was resourced and encouraged with a view to increasing both the area's wealth and its self-esteem, and Brixton also benefited from the appointment of Barry Thorley, a black member of the Archbishops' Commission, as Vicar of St Matthew's; Thorley is now Team Rector of Thamesmead. Another venture, which made an important if short-lived contribution, was the setting up of the College of St Simon of Cyrene in Wandsworth to encourage black leadership within the Church; its first Principal was Sihon Goodrich, who later became Bishop of the Windward Islands. The initiatives launched as a consequence of the publication of Faith in the City continue to this day, coordinated now under the auspices of Urban Umbrella.

Another important development during the early years of Bowlby's episcopacy was that the diocese got bigger. Because of the ancient links between the Archbishops of Canterbury and their palace at Addington, the area around Croydon had long been a part of Canterbury Diocese, even though for more than a century it had been cut off from East Kent by an intervening arm of the Diocese of Rochester. In 1985 this enclave was transferred to the Diocese of Southwark where it logically belonged, and with it the post of Suffragan Bishop of Croydon. Bowlby himself had been a Croydon incumbent prior to his elevation to Newcastle, so he already knew the area well. Southwark Diocese was redrawn as three Areas instead of two, with the Woolwich Area ceding to the Croydon Area the rural parts of Surrey, and Kingston ceding to it the London Borough of Sutton. Bowlby appointed as his first Bishop of Croydon the Archdeacon of Southwark, Wilfred Wood. Wood was well qualified for the post having already served within the diocese as vicar, rural dean, honorary canon and archdeacon, and the symbolism of the appointment was also widely welcomed since it was generally thought to be about time that England had its first black bishop (see page 35). Wood devoted much of his time to the development of race relations both nationally and within the diocese; he chaired the World Council of Churches Programme to Combat Racism and was a member both of the Archbishops' Commission on Urban Priority Areas and the Royal Commission on Criminal Procedure. In 2003 he was voted second place in the BBC's Top Black Briton contest, after Mary Seacole.

Hall and Wood were not Bowlby's only senior appointments, and he also found jobs for two prolific theological authors; Peter Selby, who had earlier been a lecturer at SOC, was made Bishop of Kingston, and David Edwards, the former managing editor of the SCM Press and publisher of "Honest to God", was made Provost. Shortly before his retirement Edwards asked for a sabbatical because he wanted to write yet another book, and Bowlby slyly responded by saying, "Surely, David, your whole career has been a sabbatical". In August 1989, in the Thames just north of the cathedral, a pleasure boat called the Marchioness was rammed by a dredger called the Bowbelle. The cathedral hosted a memorial service for all the partygoers who had been killed at which Archbishop Runcie presided, and a commemorative plaque was inlaid into the floor. The accident resulted in significant improvements being made to the river's rescue services, and also in the setting up of a system of emergency support services in which the diocese participates.

Bowlby retired in 1991 and was succeeded by Roy Williamson, an Ulsterman born into a Belfast family of fourteen children and baptised into the Church of Ireland. He was a superb communicator, assisted both by his Irish blarney and by his provenance from outside the English social hierarchy. Whereas Bowlby, though always a conscientious pastor, had had to work hard to overcome his inherited *hauteur*, Williamson had no such problem. He was able to converse easily with people from all parts of the diocese and to entertain them from his inexhaustible repertoire of anecdotes, and he was also in constant demand as an episcopal spokesman on radio and television. He arrived from being Bishop of Bradford, a diocese which has no suffragan, and he discovered that Southwark's Area system introduced by his predecessor had in some respects written him out of a role. He responded not by seeking to claw back any of the authority which his predecessor had delegated, but by developing new forms of episcopal activity; he started writing personally to all the diocese's incumbents on the anniversaries of their appointments, and he also undertook a series of lengthy walks, for example crossing all the Thames bridges from Tower Bridge to Richmond and visiting all the South Bank churches along the way.

Williamson also brought with him from Bradford an expertise in race relations, having developed there good working relationships with West Yorkshire's large and various communities of Muslims. It was, however, with the Afro-Caribbeans of South London that his skills were put most rigorously to the test. On 22 April 1993, a black teenager called Stephen Lawrence was stabbed to death at a bus stop in Eltham. Williamson supported a campaign to bring his alleged killers to justice, and welcomed the decision of the incoming Labour Government in 1997 to establish an inquiry into the case under the chairmanship of Sir William Macpherson. He was also very aware that the Church of England was almost as vulnerable to the charge of institutional racism as the Metropolitan Police, and he was instrumental in launching the process, completed under his successor, which led to the invitation to the Commission for Racial Equality to examine procedures within the diocese and to make recommendations on how the contributions of black clergy and parishioners might be better acknowledged and valued.

The most far reaching structural change that happened during Williamson's episcopacy, however, was the ordination of women to the priesthood (see page 45). The Movement for the Ordination of Women (MOW) had been particularly active within Southwark Diocese ever since its foundation in 1979, and both Bowlby and Williamson had been overtly sympathetic to its cause. It had been a Southwark diocesan motion in

Women's Ordination, Southwark Cathedral 1994

November 1984 which had launched the process that led directly to the momentous debate in General Synod exactly a decade later, and during the course of that debate Williamson spoke passionately in support of women's ordination. The voting was very close but the motion was nonetheless carried, and at Pentecost 1994 nearly one hundred women, in three separate batches, were ordained priest in Southwark Cathedral. Inevitably there were some clergy within the diocese who opposed the measure, some resigning with financial compensation and some transferring to membership of the Roman Catholic Church, but women's ministry was broadly welcomed, and the first generation of women priests were well supported in establishing themselves in their new role. One woman who did not put herself forward for ordination, on the grounds that she had fought too hard and was now too old, was Una Kroll, the first woman to train on SOC.

Williamson's successor, in 1998, was Tom Butler, who had been appointed Archdeacon of Northolt by Gerald Ellison, then Bishop of London, at the young age of forty, and later Bishop first of Willesden and then of Leicester. Leicester, like Bradford, is a diocese with a substantial Asian population, so Butler was as aware as Williamson had been of the problems that result from the white population's residual unconscious xenophobia, including that of the most liberal of Christians. He took forward Williamson's initiative in addressing institutional racism within the institutions of the Church, and oversaw the publication in 2000 of the report of a Panel of Inquiry chaired by Sir Herman Ouseley, the Chairman of the Commission for Racial Equality. He then appointed Delbert Sandiford to manage the implementation of the report's recommendations. But if it had been women's ordination that had dominated Williamson's episcopacy, the issue which dominated the early years of Butler's was homosexuality. Up till 1967 homophile sex had been a criminal offence, though one commentator had said at the time that what people found difficult was not the concept of homosexual activity as such, but any requirement to have to think about it. This reluctance to think about it had meant that there had been very little discussion of it within the Church up till the 1980s; Mervyn Stockwood had covertly allowed homosexual clergy into the diocese, particularly into the poorer areas along the riverbank where it was traditionally difficult to recruit clergy with families, and he had covertly encouraged homosexual clergy to cohabit with their partners in long-term stable relationships. This policy had been given low key support by the Gloucester Report of 1979, which concluded that there were "circumstances in which individuals may justifiably choose to enter into a homosexual relationship with the hope of enjoying a companionship and physical expression of sexual love similar to that found in marriage", but the report, though debated, was never institutionally approved. Then, during Margaret Thatcher's 1980s, came "family values" and a general backlash against social liberalism and tolerant inclusivism; AIDS was beginning to impact upon homosexual activity, Section 28 of the Local Government Act was passed with a view to prohibiting local authorities from "promoting" homosexuality, and the General Synod in 1987 passed a motion affirming that "homosexual genital acts fall short of God's ideal and are to be met by a call to repentance and the exercise of compassion".

In 1991 the House of Bishops issued a statement entitled "Issues in Human Sexuality" which addressed the issue by making a distinction, probably for the first time, between the behaviour of the laity and the behaviour of clergy. The bishops proclaimed that, though they could not "commend a loving, faithful and in intention lifelong homophile partnership as being as faithful a reflection of God's purposes in creation as the heterophile", they did "not reject those who sincerely believe it is God's call to them", adding "we stand alongside them in the fellowship of the Church, all alike dependent on the undeserved grace of God". Clergy, however, they said "cannot claim the liberty to enter into sexually active homosexual relationships". In 1998 episcopal opposition to homosexual activity was made even stronger in a resolution agreed by the Lambeth Conference, in which the gathered bishops "rejected all homosexual activity as incompatible with Scripture", saying that they could not "advise the legitimising or blessing of same-sex unions, nor ordaining those involved in same-gender unions". This stance was challenged in 2003 when Richard Harries, Bishop of Oxford, announced the appointment of Jeffrey John, Canon Theologian of Southwark Cathedral, as his Suffragan Bishop of Reading. John had written in defence of monogamous same-sex relationships and was himself in such a relationship, though the relationship was no longer sexually active. Butler supported the appointment on the grounds that John, though homosexual, was celibate and therefore not excluded by the canons of "Issues in Human Sexuality". The appointment nonetheless encountered significant hostility, particularly from Evangelicals, but it seemed for a while that Harries and Rowan Williams, the newly appointed Archbishop of Canterbury, were prepared to face down the opposition. But then the Archbishop of Nigeria announced that he would secede from the Anglican Communion if the appointment went ahead, and Williams, in the interests of Anglican unity, required John's withdrawal. A few weeks later, however, unity was again put under strain by the election of Gene Robinson, a homosexual in an active relationship and also a divorcee, as Bishop of the American Diocese of New Hampshire. John moved on to become Dean of St Albans in July 2004.

Butler's contribution to the debate, in January 2004, was to arrange one of his cathedral study days at which the issue of homosexuality was rehearsed and discussed in its entirety and from every perspective. This event was one of a series of such discussions, all of which took over the whole cathedral and involved a high proportion of the diocese's clergy. One, in 2001, entitled "God, Pure and Applied", had been addressed by Butler himself, drawing on his own mathematical and scientific background as well as on a range of literary and mystical theology. Another, arranged two years later to celebrate the fortieth anniversary of the publication of "Honest to God", had attempted to evaluate the long-term impact of South Bank Religion on theological thinking within the diocese.

Butler introduced into Southwark the practice which he had learned from Bishop Ellison of appointing clergy with perceived potential to senior positions at a comparatively young age, for example Christine Hardman as Archdeacon of Lewisham, Danny Kajumba as Archdeacon of Reigate, Richard Cheetham as Bishop of Kingston, and Nick Baines as Bishop of Croydon. He also took forward and developed the diocesan Area system which had been introduced by Bishop Bowlby, and gave it a more coherent functional structure which included enhanced scope for more effective and more personal episcopal oversight and pastoral care of the clergy by the Area bishops. He introduced arrangements under which all benefices were to be visited by the Area bishop every four years who would, as part of it, conduct a ministerial review for all licensed clergy, looking at their hopes and aspirations, their vision of the parish, and the ways in which their ministry might best be developed. Then, in subsequent years, the clergy would be seen by their archdeacon or by one of a group of trained lay people, drawn from all church and ethnic backgrounds, who would thus ensure ministerial review for everyone on an annual basis. These arrangements were welcomed by the clergy, and have since been used as a model by other dioceses. Butler's vision was of a dedicated ministry to people whoever they were and wherever they might be, supported by a structure capable of changing as circumstances changed. One aspect of this vision was the paying of the parish share, involving the archdeacons and a lay finance team, to ensure equality of ministry between the poorer and the more affluent parts of the diocese, to the enrichment of everybody's continuing contribution.

A Centennial Overview, 1905-2005

Charting the hundred years from 1905 to 2005 has required telling the story of the Church of England's decline, a decline reckoned in terms of numbers, in terms of social esteem, and in terms of political influence. Accurate statistics computing bottoms on pews are difficult to come by, but the best estimate is that church attendance during the century fell by about two thirds. Most of this drop happened during two short periods, the aftermath of World War I, and the late 1960s. History has definitively shown that the First World War was not, as many hoped and believed at the time, the "war to end all wars", but it was without a doubt the illusion to end all illusions. God was prayed in aid by both sides in the conflict and, for both sides, God comprehensively failed to deliver on what was being asked. The result was that people in droves turned angrily away, rejecting him because of his perceived gross mismanagement of the world order. They stopped seeing religion as a necessary underpinning for the fabric of society, they stopped seeing church attendance as a requirement of social convention, and they stopped seeing the clergy as the guardians of any sort of moral authority. Alternative value systems started being proffered and accepted, in the first instance everything implied by idealistic secular socialism. The Second World War was very different from the First. People came back to church with much more realistic expectations, and stayed there throughout the 1950s, but during the 1960s new and different alternative value systems were discovered, first an irresponsible hedonism, and later consumerism.

People stopped coming to church once again, but this time not because they had turned away from God, but because they could no longer see the point. They discovered they had better things to do on a Sunday morning. Gradually the Christian stories started being forgotten and Christianity's values became displaced, not because they were being consciously rejected but because, unconsciously, it seemed no longer necessary that they be taken into account. Almost certainly, however, the national decline in the Church of England's prestige and numbers has been less within the Diocese of Southwark than elsewhere. Some of this relative success has been demographic, with South London congregations constantly being swelled by immigrants from the Caribbean and from Africa, and some of it has been economic, with an increasing share of London's wealth spilling over to its southern bank to the betterment of diocesan finances. And some of it has been due to the quality of Church leadership, both leadership within the diocesan hierarchy, and also the leadership of the clergy within the parishes of the sort which Bishop Butler is now striving to foster.

This brief survey of the history of the Diocese of Southwark has used as its framework the episcopacy of its nine bishops. This is helpful in a number of ways especially in that it provides a focus and convenient chapter headings, but it is extremely unhelpful in the ways that really matter. And perhaps even writing a history is unhelpful. The Church of England south of London's river is a faith community, and what matters most about a faith community is its shared recognition of the love of God as the means of redemption both for individuals and for society. This recognition is celebrated in personal prayer and in communal worship, and what matters about personal prayer and communal worship is that both should happen, and should happen with commitment and integrity. The contexts within which they occur, and the formats which are used, are only of secondary importance. The faith life of individuals is enriched and enhanced and disciplined by being shared, and this sharing happens in the first instance within church congregations. And the faith life of church congregations is enriched and enhanced and disciplined by happening within a hierarchy of groupings, within deaneries, archdeaconries, areas, dioceses and provinces. At each stage up the hierarchy there is a subtle but significant shift of emphasis, away from the fervour of felt commitment and towards something more rational, more negotiated, and more political, and more prone to the influence of charismatic leaders. This negotiation, this politics, and this leadership is important, and interesting, and it is the stuff which historians are trained to track, but its primary purpose is as no more than the provision of an enabling framework for the inner life of the spirit. And the inner life of the spirit is rarely recorded in the archives. All that the historian can do is acknowledge its existence, and give thanks for it, and recognise the extent to which it has permeated and informed the Diocese of Southwark's first hundred years.

AFTERWORD

by Canon Eric James

The celebration of a centenary says something about memory; about, not least, its marvel and its mystery. Now that I'm in my eightieth year, I look back on people I've known in Southwark over a period of sixty-five of its hundred years.

It was Dr Edgar Tom Cook, the cathedral organist, who first welcomed me to Southwark Cathedral, when I applied to be deputy organist in 1940 when I was only fifteen. "Cookie" said I was a bit too young to be deputy organist, but he took me on as one of his pupils, and he gave me a lesson on the cathedral organ once a week, up till the time when "enemy action" forced us to transfer to Guy's Hospital Chapel. I would walk to the cathedral or to Guy's for my lesson from the riverside wharf where I was then working, now the site of the Globe Theatre. In 1944 Cuthbert Bardsley, appointed Provost of the Cathedral a few days earlier, came up into the organ loft and chatted with me, and so began a friendship which lasted till his death. A couple of years later, Bishop Bertram Simpson and a clutch of canons interviewed me as a Southwark ordinand, and I went off to King's College, London, starting there with a year at night school after work.

Geoffrey Beaumont, my predecessor both as Chaplain of Trinity College Cambridge and as Vicar of St George's Camberwell, also gave me a memorable introduction to Southwark. We first met during the war when he was on leave as a chaplain in the Royal Marines. A friend of mine, an ordinand in the Marines, had suggested that I meet Geoffrey, and we agreed to meet at St John's Waterloo where he had earlier been a curate and to which he had returned for his leave. On my way there I heard music and singing coming from a pub in the parish, the "Waterman's Arms", on the site of what is now the Royal Festival Hall. I pushed open the door and saw Geoffrey, in his cassock, sitting at the piano with a pint pot on the top of it. He was surrounded by a couple of dozen Southern Railway porters, all women in dungarees, singing to his accompaniment. It was in 1959 that I was interviewed as Geoffrey's successor as Vicar of St George's; the newly appointed bishop, Mervyn Stockwood, had told Geoffrey he could leave St George's if he was able to persuade me to become his successor. The first question that the two St George's churchwardens asked me was memorable, "do you believe that it's the vicar's job to order the hoop-la stalls for the garden fete? It's our fete tomorrow, and the last vicar forgot to order them". I asked them what THEY thought; it seemed to me to be an important part of the answer.

I shall never forget the first baptism I conducted at St George's. The infant was named Olayemi Olusola Odanye; I had to learn his name in order to pronounce it, and it has stayed with me ever since. He was the son of a Nigerian medical student living in crowded accommodation on the edge of the parish. The St George's congregation warmly welcomed the family, and we all gathered together for photographs on the steps of the church, all the Nigerians in national dress. Nearly forty years later I recorded some broadcasts for the BBC World Service, and in one of them I described Olayemi's baptism. I then flew off to Madagascar, journeying in the steps of Bishop Trevor Huddleston, and it was there that I listened to my broadcast. When I returned, I was astonished to receive letters both from Olayemi, by then a doctor in Nigeria, and from his father, who had retired there. They'd both heard the broadcast, and they both recounted to me all that had happened to them since the baptism in 1959.

I could fill a book with such Southwark memories. Those I have already recounted will serve to underline the claim I made in my opening sentence that "the celebration of a centenary says something about the significance of memory, about its marvel and its mystery". Whatever else has changed during the past century, the nature of memory has not. Yet it's not easy to say what memory is. We talk of having a "good memory", which means we are able to recall particular events and people. Yet what IS memory? It's nothing like a toe or a tooth that can be touched. It's more like an activity than an object, or rather it's a vast number of complex inter-related activities and processes. The Oxford Dictionary calls it "a faculty residing in a particular individual". Curiously, it was someone born within the diocese, or rather in 1903 just before the diocese came into being, Bob Hope, born in Eltham, who, in 1937, scored a great hit with his song "Thanks for the Memory". And maybe a major part of our centenary celebration should begin there, with thanks for the memory, or memories.

As I've said, memory isn't simple. It involves learning, retaining, selecting, recalling, and forgetting, because we can't possibly remember everything that flashes up on the screen of our memory every minute, every second. But somehow we remember SOME things. We eliminate all but a special selection, so as not to be overwhelmed and confused by a mass of memories. That surely is part of the marvel of memory, a part which is particularly apparent on an anniversary like a centenary. One of the first poems I remember learning at school was by Shelley, "Music when soft voices die vibrates in the memory". One of my most vivid Southwark memories is of Kathleen Ferrier, at the end of the war, singing Bach's St Matthew Passion in the cathedral; her soft voice still vibrates in my memory. Already, by recounting some of my memories of Southwark, I have underlined the truth of G.K.Chesterton's assertion that "for anything to be real, it must be local". My Southwark memories are all related to a particular person, place and time.

So far, I have referred mainly to pleasant memories, but of course memories are often painful. The sight of Southwark, not least its cathedral, after an air raid, still lingers painfully. And there are other aspects of memory which are painful to recall; life in any diocese is rarely all roses, and there are some memories we wish we could forget. Guilt, the need for forgiveness, and memory all go together. In my eightieth year, I'm also aware of what are now called "senior moments", the loss of memory; things once vivid become clouded by the mists of time. Many aged people these days are somewhat scared that their life will end with Alzheimer's Disease, with such a loss of memory that will mean the loss of identity. Perhaps it's worth asserting, here and now, that we will all continue to exist in the memory and love of God.

The centenary of a diocese is, not least, another opportunity to relate our Christian faith afresh to memory. The marvel and the mystery of memory leads us to wonder and to thankfulness. A brief list of some of the verses of the Bible which speak of memory may help us to prepare the centenary of Southwark:

We will remember the name of the Lord our God. Ps 20:7

Bless the Lord, O my soul, and forget not all his benefits. Ps 102:2

I thank my God on every remembrance of you. Phil 1:3

Peter remembered the words of Jesus. Matt 26:75

Remember my bonds. Col 4:18

Remember how short my time is. Ps 69:47

Lord, remember me when you come into your Kingdom. Luke 23:42

Do this in remembrance of me. Luke 22:19, I Cor 11:24

Our memory is involved in thanksgiving, intercession, worship, forgiveness, and in our recollections of the love of God and of our fellow human beings. When I think of the people I've known in Southwark over the past sixty or so years, many of whom I "love but see no longer", how should I, how should WE, remember them at this centennial time? Again, there are unforgettable phrases in the Bible for us to remember:

Be assured that I am with you always. Matt 18:20

In him we live, and move, and have our being. Acts 17:18

It is surely important, with people like the sixteenth century bishop Lancelot Andrewes who lies buried in our cathedral, to see Southwark's centenary in a larger room than solely a single century. Maybe some simple prayer should conclude this Afterword, which we can all say over and over again. In the end, we "do this", we keep our centenary, "in remembrance". We "thank God on every remembrance". I've already mentioned Bob Hope's great hit in 1937, his song "Thanks for the Memory". That very human phrase can also become a heartfelt prayer as we cast our minds back over the past hundred years:

Thanks for the memory

SOURCES AND ACKNOWLEDGEMENTS

Very little archival research has gone into this booklet. It is based rather on an examination of secondary sources and on the reminiscences of people who were around at the time, or whose forbears have passed down stories to them.

I have drawn on the following books, and should like to express my gratitude to their authors:

Bogle, Jeremy, "South Bank Religion", Hatcham Press, London, 2002

Clarke, Peter, "Hope and Glory - Britain 1900-1990", Penguin Press, Harmondsworth, 1996

De-la-Noy, Michael, "Mervyn Stockwood - A Lonely Life", Mowbray, London, 1996

Hebbert, Michael, "London, World City", Wiley and Sons, Chichester, 1998

Fryer, Peter, "Staying Power - The History of Black People in Britain", Humanities Press, Atlantic Highlands, NJ USA, 1984

James, Eric, "Bishop John A.T.Robinson - Scholar, Pastor, Prophet", Collins, London, 1987

Pevsner, Nikolaus and Cherry, Bridget, "The Buildings of England, London 2, South", Penguin Books, Harmondsworth, 1983

Sheppard, David, "Steps Along Hope Street - My Life in Cricket, the Church and the Inner City", Hodder and Stoughton, London, 2002

Stephenson, Gwendolen, "Edward Stuart Talbot", SPCK, London, 1936

Smyth, Charles, "Cyril Foster Garbett", Hodder and Stoughton, London, 1959

I am also grateful to the following people who have shared with me their memories and experience:

Canon Ian Ainsworth Smith, Ven Martin Baddeley, Linda Borthwick, Rt Revd Colin Buchanan, Rt Revd Richard Cartwright, Canon Peter Challen, Ven David Gerrard, Revd Keith Holt, Revd Patrick Rosheuvel, Gwen Rymer, Delbert Sandiford, Revd Grahame Shaw, Revd Dr Jane Steen, Revd Malcolm Torry, and Rt Revd Wilfred Wood.

I am particularly grateful to Rt Revd Tom Butler for his authoritative enthusiasm and support, to Canons Eric James and Jeffrey John for their informed guidance throughout the project, to Janet Woolley who helped to put it all together and to Wendy Robins and Canon Andrew Nunn who assisted me at various stages of the process.

The portraits of the bishops are from the diocesan archive. The black and white photographs are all from the collection of the Southwark Local Studies Library in Borough High Street, and are reproduced with its kind permission, apart from the portrait of the Jamaican family on page 31 which is reproduced by the kind permission of the Lambeth Archive at the Minet Library in Knatchbull Road. The colour photographs illustrating the development of South London domestic architecture were taken by me.

This book was designed, typeset and printed by Tony James in Colchester.

TIME CHART

	Bishops of Southwark	Archbishops of Canterbury	Prime Ministers
1895			Lord Salisbury (Con and Unionist)
1896		Frederick Temple	
1902			Arthur Balfour (Con and Unionist)
1903		Randall Davidson	
1905	Edward Talbot		Henry Campbell-Bannerman (Lib)
1908			Herbert Asquith (Lib)
1911	Hubert Burge		
1916			David Lloyd George (Lib)
1919	Cyril Garbett		
1922			Andrew Bonar Law (Con)
1923			Stanley Baldwin (Con)
1924			Ramsay MacDonald (Lab then Nat)
1928		Cosmo Lang	
1932	Richard Parsons		
1935			Stanley Baldwin (Con)
1937			Neville Chamberlain (Con)
1940			Winston Churchill (Coalition)
1942	Bertram Simpson	William Temple	
1945		Geoffrey Fisher	Clement Attlee (Lab)
1951			Winston Churchill (Con)
1955			Anthony Eden (Con)
1957			Harold Macmillan (Con)
1959	Mervyn Stockwood		
1961		Michael Ramsey	
1963			Alec Douglas-Home (Con)
1964			Harold Wilson (Lab)
1970			Edward Heath (Con)
1974		Donald Coggan	Harold Wilson (Lab)
1976			James Callaghan (Lab)
1979		Robert Runcie	Margaret Thatcher (Con)
1980	Ronald Bowlby		
1990			John Major (Con)
1991	Roy Williamson	George Carey	
1997			Tony Blair (Lab)
1998	Tom Butler		
2003		Rowan Williams	